Old Florence And Modern Tuscany

Janet Ross

OLD FLORENCE
AND MODERN TUSCANY

BOOKS BY THE SAME AUTHOR

FLORENTINE VILLAS

Illustrated with Photogravure Reproductions of Zocchi's Engravings of the Villas; of sixteen Medals in the Bargello; and of a Death Mask of Lorenzo the Magnificent. Also with text illustrations by NELLY ERICHSEN. Also a Large Paper Edition. Imperial 4to, £3 3*s.* net.

LEAVES FROM OUR TUSCAN KITCHEN; OR HOW TO COOK VEGETABLES

With Photogravure Frontispiece. Foolscap 8vo, 2*s.* 6*d.* net. [*Third Edition.*

LETTERS FROM THE EAST, 1837–1857

By HENRY JAMES ROSS. Edited by his Wife, JANET ROSS. With Photogravure Portraits, and Illustrations from Photographs. Demy 8vo, 12*s.* 6*d.* net.

In preparation

FLORENTINE PALACES

AND

MODERN TUSCANY

BY

JANET ROSS

NEW YORK: E. P. DUTTON & CO.

1904

OLD FLORENCE

AND

MODERN TUSCANY

BY

JANET ROSS

WITH ILLUSTRATIONS

LONDON: J. M. DENT & CO.
NEW YORK: E. P. DUTTON & CO.
1904

PREFACE

SEVERAL of the following papers have already been published, and I owe to the courtesy of Messrs. Macmillan, Messrs. Longman, Mr. Edward Arnold, and Mr. Murray, the permission to reprint them.*

Some may think my pictures of the Tuscan peasants flattering and highly coloured. I can only say that I have lived among them for thirty-four years, and that nowhere does the golden rule, "Do as you would be done by," hold good so much as in Italy.

I could tell many stories of their ready kindliness, for, as my mother says in her *Letters from Egypt*, I "sit among the people," and do not "make myself big," a proceeding an Italian resents as much as an Arab.

* "Old Florence and Modern Tuscany,"[1] "The Dove of Holy Saturday," "Vintaging in Tuscany," "Oil-making in Tuscany," "Volterra"—*Macmillan's Magazine.* "A September Day in the Valley of the Arno," "The Brotherhood of Pity in Florence"—*English Illustrated Magazine.* "Popular Songs of Tuscany"—*Fraser's Magazine.* "Virgil and Agriculture in Tuscany"—*Longman's Magazine.* "A Stroll in Boccaccio's Country"—*The National Review.* "A Domestic Chaplain of the Medici"—*Monthly Review.*

JANET ROSS.

[1] Only partly reprinted as "Old Florence."

CONTENTS

LIST OF ILLUSTRATIONS

OLD FLORENCE
AND
MODERN TUSCANY

THE BROTHERHOOD OF PITY AT FLORENCE

MOST visitors to Florence have seen the brethren of the Misericordia bound on some mission of mercy, gliding silently—black ghosts carrying a black catafalque—through the city. All heads are uncovered as they pass, and the most ribald and uncouth carter draws his mules on one side to give more room.

No wonder the Florentines are proud of their Confraternity, the finest charitable institution that ever was founded. Anyone can give money, but the brethren give personal fatigue, and are often exposed to infection. Neither winter snow nor burning summer sun stops the devoted band. Three times a day the bell of the Misericordia Chapel, in the Piazza del Duomo, rings to call those of the Confraternity whose turn it is to carry sick poor to the hospital. Ten brethren usually go with each litter, under the orders of a Capo di Guardia, who is distinguished by a bag tied round his waist containing brandy, cough lozenges, and the key of a drawer under the litter in which is a drinking-cup, a stole, a crucifix, the ritual, and some holy water, in case the sick person should die on the way. The long overcoat and the cowl with two holes for the eyes are made of black cotton, and black gaiters are worn so that the brethren may not be recognised by the colour of their trousers. The cowl may only be thrown back outside the city gates and in certain specified streets, and if it rains hard or the sun is powerful, a black felt hat is worn over it. Four brethren carry the litter, which weighs about 180 lbs., and the reserve men keep one hand under the poles in case a bearer should stumble or fall. A slight tap on the pole is the signal for changing bearers, and this is so skilfully done that the sick or wounded are never shaken. The fresh men say as they relieve the others, "May God reward you!" and the answer is: "Go in peace!"

If they have to go some distance, sixteen brethren are told off for service, and should the case be a very bad one, a brother walks on either side of the litter to watch the invalid's face or feel his pulse.

Should the door of the house be too small to admit the litter, the Capo di Guardia and six brethren go to the sick-room. Tenderly and carefully they carry the invalid on a thick quilted coverlid to the litter, and the arched top is opened against the street so that curious passers-by should not see the sick person. Before leaving the room, the Capo di Guardia leaves a small sum on the table, in obedience to a legacy left for that purpose to the Confraternity by two pious citizens in long past days, and if the invalid is the bread-winner, or the poverty of the family evident, the Capo di Guardia begs the brethren to do yet another charity, and holding his hat together like a bag he goes from one to another to collect alms. He asks the sick person to whom the money is to be given, and, without counting, pours the contents of his hat into their hands. The members of the Misericordia take it by turn to go at stated hours to the houses of sick people to change their linen, or to sit up at night with those who are too poor to pay a nurse. In maladies like rheumatic fever, when the slightest touch is agony, they are often called by rich folk to lift an invalid—so gentle and sure from long habit is their touch. No brother is allowed to accept anything—money or food—save a glass of water, in any house.

Someone is always on guard at the Misericordia Chapel, and if an accident occurs a message is sent there to call a litter. Then the great bell of Giotto's Tower, just opposite the chapel, is tolled in a peculiar way—twice for an accident, three times for a death—to call the brethren who are on the list for that day.

Twice it has happened to me that a shopman has

left his wife to serve in the shop, while he hastily threw on his cloak and ran out of the door. The first time, being new to Florence, I thought the man had gone mad. My face, I suppose, showed surprise, for one of the customers said, "Eh, signora, don't you hear the bell?—an accident."

A member of one of the oldest and most noble families of Florence told me his experience with the Misericordia. One evening in the old Ghetto, a poor woman, on the eve of her confinement, was lying in the room where her husband, his brother, and two children were ill with typhoid fever, and the Misericordia had been called to take her to the hospital. She lived on the ninth story of the tower of the old Tosa Palace, up a precipitous and narrow staircase with many turnings. The question arose how to carry her down in safety, and was solved by my friend. He crept under the quilt, which was held by four bearers, and on hands and knees he went backwards down the long staircase, with the poor woman on his back. It took nearly half an hour to reach the litter in the street, and the bearer was stiff for many days afterwards. To the baby boy, who came into the world three hours after the woman reached the hospital, he stood godfather, saw to the child's education, and made a man of him.

According to tradition, the Misericordia was founded in 1240, when Florence supplied the world with cloth, and many porters were employed to carry the bales from the weavers to the dyers, and from thence to the merchants' warehouses. The men took refuge from summer sun and winter wind in some unused cellars belonging to the Adimari, in the Piazza del Duomo. (All Florentines will tell you that some shelter is necessary against the wind which always blows round and round the cathedral in hot pursuit of the devil, who, being clever and utterly shameless, eludes his enemy by slipping in at one side door of the Duomo and out at the other.) The porters were much given to cursing and swearing, to this day a well-known Tuscan vice, so one Piero Borsi, an old and devout man, scandalised by his companions' blasphemous talk, proposed that everyone who took the names of God or the Holy Virgin in vain, should be obliged to put a crazia into a box by way of penance. They adhered to this idea, and, as an old writer quaintly says, "much time having passed in this devout exercise, large sums accumulated," and old Piero suggested that six litters should be made, one for each quarter of the city, and that every porter should undertake to devote six days in the year to carrying the sick, or those who fell from scaffolds, were murdered, drowned, or hurt in the streets, to hospital. For every journey they were to receive a giulio. This proposal met with universal approbation, and was carried out.

Count L. Passerini, in his exhaustive work on the charitable institutions of Florence,[1] ridicules this old tradition, and quotes the learned and saintly Archbishop Antonino of Florence in support of his opinion that the Misericordia was an offshoot of another confraternity, the Laudesi of Or-San-Michele, founded in 1292. He believes that the separation took place in 1326, during the pestilence which broke out in the city owing, old writers say, to the many unburied corpses of the soldiers who fell at the battle of Altopascio, whereby the air was corrupted. So many people died that the Republic forbade the tolling of the passing bell, or the publication of the number of deaths.

In 1340 there was another outbreak, which chiefly attacked the very poor, and then came the great plague of 1348, so eloquently described by Boccaccio. The historian Giovanni Villani died of it, and his son Matteo reports that three persons perished out of every five. Palmieri says: "Igneus vapor magnitudine horribile boreali moveus regione, magno aspicietinui terrore per cœlum dilabitur: et quidam scribunt hoc eodem anno quosdam bestiolas multiplicato munere in Oriente e cœlo cecidisse, quarum corruptio et fœtor pestilentiam intulerant." Florence was strewn with

[1] *Storia degli Stabilimenti di Beneficenza e d'Instruzione Elementar Gratuita della Città di Firenze*, da Luigi Passerini.—(Le Monnier Firenze, 1853.)

corpses, and no sound save the measured tread of the brethren of the Misericordia broke the silence of the streets. They behaved like heroes, buried the dead, took charge of the orphans, distributed food and clothes to the needy, and the Florentines showed their gratitude by bequeathing to the Confraternity 35,000 golden florins.

In 1363 the plague once more decimated the unfortunate city, and Matteo Villani, like his father before him, died of it, as did the valorous soldier, Pier Farnese, who was buried with great pomp in the Cathedral. The Misericordia again braved infection, when, as Dante says, Florence—

> Was chaste and sober,
> And her citizens were content
> With unrobed jerkins.

Men too were conscientious in those days, as a story Count Passerini quotes goes to show. A certain Florentine, Neri Boscoli, who had been a banker in Naples, and bore an evil name as a usurer, left a large fortune to the Confraternity. So the captains of the Misericordia hesitated about accepting a legacy stained with the tears of the poor. They called the first theologians of Florence together to advise them, and unanimously the holy men decided that the captains might accept the legacy—what had been taken from the poor would thus be given back to them—but that they ought to return to any who could produce absolute proof the amount that Boscoli had extorted by exorbitant usury. This was done, and all men were satisfied.

Besides exercising charity, the Misericordia were before their age in ideas of municipal government. A century and a half before any such thing was thought of in other European cities, the captains met together on February 20th, 1407, and decreed that their notary should take exact note—in a large book to be made for the purpose—of every child born in the city, and of every person baptised in San Giovanni. Till then the priest had kept a primitive register of the number by dropping a black bean for every male, a white for every female, into a box, whereby mistakes often arose. Unfortunately the old books of the Confraternity perished in the great inundation of 1557, when the Arno did so much damage.

In the fourteenth and fifteenth centuries Florence was visited at frequent intervals by the plague, and when reading the accounts of the old historians one wonders that the human race was not exterminated. The Misericordia continued to exercise their charitable mission until they fell a victim to the intrigues of a Medici. Cosimo di Giovanni de' Medici was Camarlingo, or overseer of the Confraternity of Santa Maria del Bigallo, which had once been famed for good deeds and enriched by large legacies. But maladministration had ruined their patrimony, and odious comparisons were drawn between the two institutions. So, in 1425, Cosimo induced the Signory of Florence to order the fusion of the Misericordia with the Bigallo, and took care that the latter should be paramount in the management, especially of the funds. Abuses of all kinds crept in, the treasure which had been left for the benefit of the poor was squandered in banquets and festivities, and the Misericordia soon ceased to exist. But the memory of their self-sacrifice survived in the hearts of the people, and a small incident sufficed to resuscitate the noble charity. Filippo Tornabuoni, in his diary, relates how in 1480 a man dropped down dead in Via S. Francesco, and for days the corpse lay festering in the street, until a citizen took it on his back to the palace of the Signoria. Throwing down his load at the feet of the Gonfalonier, he said: "This comes of you and your predecessors not observing the old laws and customs." Whereupon it was determined to reconstitute the Misericordia, and the captains of the Bigallo, all citizens of high repute, met and drew up statutes which exist, with little change, to this day. They commence: "Inasmuch as Our Lord Jesus Christ, besides a number of the Apostles, instituted and ordained seventy-two disciples, who were charged to go with charity into the world, preaching and disseminating His doctrine, we order that the aforesaid number of our Confraternity and company, seventy-two, shall go into our territory of Florence, practising the work of mercy and charity; especially shall they bury the dead of the poor and miserable without retribution or guerdon, doing this solely for the love of Jesus Christ, who suffered death and passion for the love of us."

Besides the seventy-two Capi di Guardia, thirty of whom belong to the priesthood and forty to the laity, there are some hundreds of Giornanti (day-workers), Stracciafogli (paper-tearers), and Buonevoglie (well-intentioned), who have no voice in the management of the Confraternity.

The Giornanti are bound to serve one day in every week, or if they cannot do this, to sleep one night in the week at the Misericordia, where there is a room with four beds. They go there at ten p.m., and cannot leave until five in the morning, when the first mass is said. The queer name of Stracciafogli comes from the old custom of tearing up thin paper slips, one of which was given to each man after he had accomplished a journey. No apprentice is admitted into the Confraternity without his master's consent, nor any youth under age, save by his father's wish. No servant in livery can belong to it, nor can any barber, hairdresser, coachman, cobbler, seller of fish or of salt meats and sausages, or any person following a trade which is considered mean or vile. No man can belong to the Misericordia who has been condemned in a court of law, or is notoriously an evil liver. Characteristic of the Italian passion for regulating everything are the innumerable laws and regulations laid down for the conduct of the brethren, and the pains and penalties for their non-observance.

There are six captains and six counsellors, eight conservators (not including the King and the Archbishop of Florence, who hold that rank by virtue of their position), a provider, a chancellor, a secretary, an overseer, and two visitors of sick brethren of the Confraternity, who distribute certain alms on the certificate of the doctor of the Misericordia. The daughters of the Capi di Guardia can compete for dowers, which are given every year, and if any of the seventy-two brethren fall into poverty they are given a small stipend every month. The conservators hold their office for life, the others change every four months, and all are chosen by lot from the seventy-two Capi di Guardia. A small annual payment gives them a right to be buried in the cemetery of the Misericordia, and to fifteen masses for the repose of their souls. When a Capo di Guardia dies his place is filled by the Giornante who has the longest service, he is in turn succeeded by the Stracciafoglio who has shown most zeal and charity.

Soon after the Misericordia had been reconstructed the plague broke out again. Bad in 1495, it was worse in 1498, when the Republic gave the Confraternity full powers to do what seemed best to them to prevent the spread of the disease. But for ten years it lingered in and around the city. The Confraternity established several hospitals, and in one,[1] near the old gate of Justice, a certain number of brethren shut themselves up with the sick and did all the nursing themselves. Between 1522 and 1528 the plague was worse than ever; sixty thousand people died. Benedetto Varchi, Bernardo Segni, and Scipione Ammirato all bear testimony to the heroic self-devotion of the Misericordia, and in 1630 during another outbreak of the plague, the Misericordia had so much to do that the bearers of a litter were reduced to two brethren, while another walked in front ringing a bell to warn passers-by to get out of the way. They abolished the ordinary mattresses in the litters and used hay or straw, which was burnt after every journey.

In 1633 came another wave of infection, which, however, soon spent itself. Pious people attributed the cessation of the sickness to the miraculous image of the famous Virgin of the Impruneta, who, in solemn procession, was carried from her hill-top into the city; but more matter-of-fact folk said it was due to a strict system of isolation inaugurated by the brethren of the Misericordia. This was the last plague in Florence, and in the archives of the Confraternity still exist the

[1] Now Montedomini, or the poor-house of Florence.

curious old books containing the names of those who were taken to the various hospitals or to the cemeteries, the deliberations of the chiefs, the sums spent in charity, and lists of things found in plague-stricken and abandoned houses.

The Misericordia has had various residences. The beautiful Loggia (del Bigallo) opposite the Baptistery was built for them by Orcagna, but fell to the Bigallo when the Misericordia took a house belonging to Tomaso Ginori in 1523. The Signoria then gave them the Church of St. Christopher in the Corso degli Adimari, where they remained until 1575, when the Grand Duke Francis I., "in order that so exemplary a work, which brings such honour to the city of Florence, should not be hid, but stand in a conspicuous and visible place," gave them the building where the Court of Trustees used to assemble on the Piazza del Duomo. Here the Misericordia still meet, and it is like suddenly stepping back several hundreds of years to attend the gathering and starting of the brethren on their charitable missions. The whole place is neatness and cleanliness itself, and in the little church is a beautiful altar-piece by Luca della Robbia, brought from the old abbey of Rocettini early in the last century. A more gracious and lovely Virgin was never fashioned by the great artist, and the Holy Child has the same wonderful expression that Raphael has given Him in the famous Dresden picture, the Sistine Madonna. A halo of cherubim surrounds the Virgin, and a saint stands on either side. In the secretary's room is a curious picture by Cigoli of the Piazza del Duomo during the great plague. There are also two works in marble by Benedetto di Majano in the oratory, a Madonna and Child, and a St. Sebastian (the patron saint of the Confraternity), which are worth seeing.

But the most interesting painting done for the Misericordia when they assembled in the Bigallo is, perforce, still there—a fresco, attributed to Giottino, of Charity, with the city of Florence at her feet. She stands erect, robed like a nun, her head crowned with a mitre bearing the mystic Thau in the centre and the words "Misericordia Domini" round the edge. Her hands are folded in prayer, and the mantle which hangs from her shoulders is ornamented with five medallions on either side representing various works of charity and Latin mottoes in praise thereof. A crowd of people kneel on either side, the men to the right, the women to the left. Interesting for the dresses and the representation of ancient Florence with the first circle of walls, this fresco would be invaluable if there existed any key to the kneeling personages, for they are indubitably portraits. It has been injured by restoration, and many of the words are illegible or mere nonsense. The date, which with the inscription has been entirely repainted, is

MCCCXLII., but Sandini, who wrote the history of the Misericordia in the eighteenth century, gives it as ten years later. When cholera devastated Florence in 1855, the brethren of the Misericordia once more came to the front, proving that the old virtues of charity and self-sacrifice still exist amongst the burghers of the city of flowers.

OLD FLORENCE

"FLORENCE within her ancient limit-mark,
Which calls her still to matin prayers and noon,
Was chaste and sober, and abode in peace.
She had no amulet, no head-tires then,
No purfled dames; no zone, that caught the eye
More than the person did. Time was not yet,
When at his daughters' births the sire grew pale,
For fear the age and dowry should exceed,
On each side, just proportion. House was none,
Void of its family; nor yet had come
Sardanapalus to exhibit feats
Of chamber prowess. Montemalo yet
O'er our suburban turret rose; as much
To be surpast in fall, as in its rising.
I saw Bellincion Berti walk abroad
In leathern girdle, and a clasp of bone;
And, with no artificial colouring on her cheeks,
His lady leave the glass. The sons I saw
Of Nerli, and of Vecchio, well content
With unrobed jerkin; and their good dames handling
The spindle and the flax. Oh, happy they!"

Thus writes Dante, in *Paradise*, about the sobriety and simplicity of dress and manners in Florence in his day; and nearly a century later G. Villani tells us:

"The citizens of Florence lived soberly, on coarse viands and at small cost; they were rude and unpolished in many customs and courtesies of life, and dressed themselves and their women in coarse cloth; many wore plain leather, without cloth over it; bonnets on their heads; and all, boots on their feet. The Florentine women were without ornament; the better sort being content with a close gown of scarlet cloth of Ypres or of camlet, tied with a girdle in the ancient mode, and a mantle lined with fur, with a hood attached to be worn on the head. The common sort of women were clad in a coarse gown of cambrai in like fashion."

Things changed soon after this, as in 1415 the sage old Florentines were obliged to draw up a series of sumptuary laws, directed against the luxury and splendour of women's dress and of marriage festivals. They declared that such magnificence was opposed to all republican laws and usages, and only served to enervate and corrupt the people. If a citizen of Florence wished to give an entertainment in honour of a guest, he had to obtain a permit from the Priors of Liberty, for which he paid ten golden florins, and also to swear that such splendour was only exhibited for the honour and glory of the city. Whoever transgressed this law was fined twenty-five golden florins. It was considered shameful to have much plate; nearly all household implements were of brass, now and then beautified by having the arms of the family in enamel upon them. These sumptuary laws were not confined to Florence. The town of Pistoja enacted similar ones in 1322; Perugia in 1333.

Phillipe le Bel promulgated sumptuary laws in France in 1310; Charles IX. in 1575; and Louis XIII. in 1614; with no greater success than the worthy old republicans.

Pandolfini, in his curious book, *Del Governo della Famiglia*, inveighs against the Florentine custom of painting the face. In his counsels to his young wife, Giovanna degli Strozzi, he says:

> "Avoid all those false appearances by which dishonest and bad women try to allure men, thinking with ointments, white lead and paint, with lascivious and immoral dress, to please men better than when adorned with simplicity and true honesty. Not only is this reprehensible, but it is most unwholesome to corrupt the face with lime, poisons, and so-called washes. See, oh, my wife, how fresh and well-looking are all the women of this house! This is because they use only water from the well as an ointment; do thou likewise, and do not plaster and whiten thy face, thinking to appear more beautiful in my eyes. Thou art fresh and of a fine colour; think not to please me by cheatery and showing thyself to me as thou art not, because I am not to be deceived; I see thee at all hours, and well I know how thou art without paint."

The Florentine ladies appear to have held their own against all these attempts to convert them to a simpler mode of life. Sachetti gives an amusing instance of their ready wit while he was Prior of the Republic.

A new judge, Amerigo degli Amerighi, came from Pesaro, and was specially ordered to see that the sumptuary laws were obeyed. He fell into disgrace for doing too little, and his defence is as follows:

> "My masters, I have worked all my life at the study of law, and now that I thought I knew something I find I know nothing; for trying to discover the forbidden ornaments worn by your women, according to the orders you gave me, I have not found in any law-book arguments such as they give. I will cite you some. I met a woman with a border, all curiously ornamented and slashed, turned over her hood; the notary said to her, 'Give me your name, for you have an embroidered border.' The good woman takes off the border, which was attached to her hood with a pin, and holding it in her hand, replies that it is a garland. Others wear many buttons down the front of their dresses; I say to one, 'You may not wear those buttons,' and she answers, 'Yes, sir, I can, for these are not buttons, but *coppelle*, and if you do not believe me, see, they have no haft, and there are no buttonholes.' The notary goes up to a third, who was wearing ermine, and says, 'How can you excuse yourself, you are wearing ermine?' and begins to write the accusation. The woman replies, 'No, do not write, for this is not ermine, but *lattizzo*' (fur of any young sucking animal). The notary asked, 'And what is this *lattizzo*?' And the woman's answer was, 'The man is a fool!'"

The widows seem to have given less trouble; but

they always took care that their dresses should be well cut and fit perfectly.

Philosophers, of course, wrote treatises on political economy, and poets satirised the different fashions of their times. Thus, in *Lodovico Adimari*, we read:

"The high-born dame now plasters all her cheeks
With paint by shovelfuls, and in curled rings
Or tortuous tresses twines her hair, and seeks
To shave with splintered glass the down that springs
On her smooth face and soft skin, till they seem
The fairest, tenderest of all tender things:
Rouge and vermilion make her red lips beam
Like rubies burning on the brow divine
Of heaven-descended Iris: jewels gleam
About her breasts, embroidered on the shrine
Of satins, silks, and velvets: like the snails,
A house in one dress on her back she trails." [1]

Cennino Cennini, a painter, and pupil of Agnolo Gaddi, the godson of Giotto, says, in his *Treatise on Painting*:

"It might be for the service of young ladies, more especially those of Tuscany, to mention some colours which they think highly of, and use for beautifying themselves; and also certain washes. But as those of Padua do not use such things, and I do not wish to make myself obnoxious to them, or to incur the displeasure of God and of Our Lady, I shall say no more on this subject. But," he continues, "if thou desirest to preserve thy complexion for a long time, I advise thee to wash thyself with water from fountains,

[1] Translated for me by Mr. J. A. Symonds.

rivers, or wells. I warn thee that if thou usest cosmetics thy face will become hideous and thy teeth black; thou wilt be old before thy time, and the ugliest object possible. This is quite enough to say on this subject."

Cennini seems, notwithstanding, to have been employed to paint people's faces, if we may judge from the following passage in the same work:

> "Sometimes you may be obliged to paint or dye flesh, faces of men and women in particular. You can mix your colours with yolk of egg; or should you wish to make them more brilliant, with oil, or liquid varnish, the strongest of all *temperas*. Do you want to remove the colours or *tempera* from the face? Take yolk of egg and rub it, a little at a time, with your hand on the face. Then take clean water, in which bran has been boiled, and wash the face; then more of the yolk of egg, and again rub the face with it; and again wash with warm water. Repeat this many times until the face returns to its original colour."

The sumptuary laws cited by the *Osservatore Fiorentino* are as follow:

> "1st. It is forbidden for any unmarried woman to wear pearls or precious stones, and married dames may only wear ornaments to the value of forty golden florins at any one time.
>
> "2nd. In the week preceding a wedding, neither bride nor bridegroom may ask to dinner or supper more than four persons not appertaining to the house.

"3rd. The brides who desire to go to church on horseback may do so, but are not to be accompanied by more than six women attendants.

"4th. On the marriage day, only sixteen women may dine in the bridegroom's house, six of the bride's family and ten of the bridegroom's, besides his mother, his sisters, and his aunts.

"5th. There may only be ten men of the family, and eight friends; boys under fourteen do not count.

"6th. During the repast, only three musicians and singers are allowed.

"7th. The dinner or supper may not consist of more than three solid dishes, but confectionery and fruit *ad libitum.*

"8th. The bride and bridegroom are allowed to invite two hundred people to witness the signing of the contract before the celebration of the marriage."

These laws, however, appear to have been of little use, to judge by the representation of the marriage procession of Boccaccio degli Adimari on the *cassone,* or marriage-chest, the painted front of which is now in the Academia delle Belle Arte, at Florence. Men and women magnificently clad are walking hand in hand, under a canopy of red and white damask, supported by poles, and stretched from the lovely little Loggia del Bigallo, past Lorenzo Ghiberti's famous doors of the baptistery of San Giovanni, to the corner of Via de' Martelli. The trumpeters of the Republic sit on the steps of the Loggia, blowing their golden trumpets ornamented with square flags, on which is emblazoned the lily of the city of Florence. Pages in gorgeous clothes, carrying gold and silver vases on their heads, are passing in and out of one of the Adimari palaces, and a man behind the musicians holds a flask of wine in his hand, just the same flask as one sees now in daily use in Tuscany. The ladies have head-dresses like large turbans; one is made of peacock's feathers, and all are sparkling with jewels.

Funerals were also of great show and splendour in those days, and their cost increased rapidily. In 1340 the funeral of Gherardo Baroncelli cost only two hundred golden florins, and about the same time that of Giotto Peruzzi five hundred; whereas, in 1377, the expenses for the burial of Monaldo, son of Messer Niccolaio d' Jacopo degli Alberti, amounted to three thousand golden florins, nearly five thousand pounds.

The following details of this magnificent affair, from the manuscript of Monaldi, may interest the curious reader:

> "Monaldo Alberti di Messer Niccolaio d' Jacopo degli Alberti, died on the 7th of August, 1377; he passed for the richest man, as regards money, in the country. He was buried on the 8th of August, in Santa Croce, with great honour of torches and wax candles. The funeral car was of red damask, and he was dressed in the same red damask, in cloth and in

cloth of gold. There were eight horsemen, one decked with the arms of the people, because he was a cavalier of the people; one with the arms of the Guelphs, because he was one of their captains; two horses were covered with big banners, on which were emblazoned the Alberti arms; one horseman had a pennant, and a casque and sword, and spurs of gold, and on the casque was a damsel with two wings; another horse was covered with scarlet, and his rider had a thick mantle of fur, lined; another horse was undraped, and his rider wore a violet cloak lined with dark fur.

"When the body was removed from the arcade of the house, there was a sermon; seventy-two torches surrounded the car, that is to say, sixty belonged to the house, and twelve to the Guelph party. A large catafalque was all furnished with torches of a pound weight; and the whole church, and the chief chapels towards the centre of the church, were full of small torches of half a pound weight, often interspersed with those of one pound. All the relations, and those of close parentage with the house of Alberti, were dressed in blood-red, and all the women who belonged to them, or had entered the family by marriage, wore the same colour. Many other families were in black. A great quantity of money was there to give away for God, etc. Never had been seen such honours. This funeral cost something like three thousand golden florins."

The Medici made no attempt to control this splendour; indeed, one of Lorenzo the Magnificent's favourite sayings was *Pane e feste tengon il popol quieto*

(Bread and shows keep the people quiet). Cosmo I. had a passion for jousts and games of all sorts, ballets on horseback, and masquerades, which were generally held in the Piazza Sta. Croce. The masquerade to celebrate the arrival of Ubaldo della Rovere, Prince of Urbino, in 1615, has been engraved by Jacques Callot, and was called the War of Love. First came the chariot of Love, surrounded with clouds, which opened showing Love and his court. Then came the car of Mount Parnassus with the Muses, Paladins, and famous men of letters. The third was the chariot of the Sun, with the twelve signs of the zodiac, the serpent of Egypt, the months and the seasons; and was surrounded by eight Ethiopian giants. The car of Thetis closed the procession, with Sirens, Nereids, and Tritons, and eight giant Neptunes, to represent the principal seas of the world.

Ferdinand II. also delighted in these shows, and several held during his reign have been engraved by Stefano della Bella and Jacques Callot.

Princess Violante of Bavaria, who, in 1689, came to marry Ferdinand, son of Cosmo III., was received with great splendour. She entered Florence by the Porta San Gallo, where a chapel had been erected for the ceremony of crowning her as she crossed the threshold of the city. The princess then seated herself on a jewelled throne, and was carried into the town under a canopy borne by a number of youths, splendidly dressed, and chosen for their beauty and high birth. After a solemn thanksgiving in the cathedral, she was escorted to the Pitti Palace by the senate and the chief people of the city. The carnival feasts that year were more magnificent than usual in her honour.

T. Rinnucini, writing to a friend in the beginning of the seventeenth century, gives the following quaint account of a wedding in his own family:

> "When the alliance was arranged, we went in person to all our near relatives, and sent servants to those of remoter kin, to give notice of the day on which the bride would leave our house in her bridal attire; so that all relations down to the third degree might accompany her to mass. At the house door, we found a company of youths, the *seraglio*, as we say, who complimented my niece, and made as though they would not allow her to quit the house until she bestowed on them rings or clasps, or some such trinkets. When she had, with infinite grace, given the usual presents, the spokesman of the party, who was the youngest, and of high family, waited on the bride, and served her as far as the church door, giving her his arm. After the marriage, we had a grand banquet, with all the relations on both sides, and the youths of the *seraglio*, who, in truth, have a right to be present at the feast."

In other descriptions of marriages about the same time, we read that during the banquet a messenger sought audience of the bride, and presented her with a basket of flowers, or a pair of scented gloves, sent by the *seraglio*, together with the rings, clasps, or other ornaments she had given them on leaving her father's house. The bridegroom, according to his means, gave the messenger thirty, forty, fifty, or if very rich, a hundred *scudi*, which the youths spent in a great feast to their companions and friends, in a masquerade, or some such entertainment.

The marriage-ring was given on another day, when there was a feast of white confectionery, followed by dancing, if the size of the house permitted it. Otherwise the company played at *giulè*, a game of cards no longer known; the name being derived, says Salvini, from the coin called *giulio*, worth fifty-six *centimes*, which was placed in a plate in the middle of the table as the stake.

At the beginning of the feast the names of the guests were read out according to their different degrees of parentage, so that all might find their places without confusion.

The bride's dower was carried in procession to the bridegroom's house, in the *cassoni*, or marriage-chests, which varied in splendour according to the riches of the family. Some were of carved wood, some inlaid, others covered with velvet ornamented with richly gilt ironwork, but the finest of all were painted by famous artists with the deeds of the ancestors of the family. The great luxury consisted in fine linen; "twenty dozen of everything," was the rule in those days, and is still adhered to among old-fashioned people in Tuscany.

It was in such a marriage-chest that the beautiful Ginevra dei Benci, whose portrait exists in the fresco by Ghirlandajo in Sta. Maria Novella, hid, while playing hide and seek the evening before her marriage. The *cassone* was of carved wood, and the heavy lid closed upon her, snapping the lock fast. All search for her was vain, and the old tale says that her fair fame suffered at the hands of malicious women, jealous of her exceeding beauty. Years afterwards, when the chest was forced open, the body of the lovely Ginevra was found, still, it is said, preserving traces of beauty, and with the peculiar scent she used yet lingering about her long, fair hair, whilst in her right hand she grasped the jewel her bridegroom had given her to fasten the front of her gown. In Florence *la bella Ginevra* still passes among the common people as the ideal type of woman's beauty.

A Domestic Chaplain of the Medici

One of the most original figures in the brilliant court of Lorenzo de' Medici was Matteo Franco.[1] Born in Florence of poor parents of the name of Della Badessa in 1447, he simply adopted his father's Christian name of Franco, as was often done in the fifteenth century, and called himself Matteo di Franco, which soon became plain Matteo Franco. As a lad he entered the Church, and some of his first efforts in poetry are sonnets addressed to the Archbishop of Florence, begging in the name of St. Peter for a cloak. In others he states that his income is but three lire a month, and that never a crumb of bread remains on the table after meals. His poverty was rendered more irksome when, after the death of his parents, he took his young sister Ginevra and an old maid to live with him. Ginevra, however, soon married a Doctor Leopardi, a converted Jew, known in Florence as "il medico della barba," or the bearded doctor, and Matteo made friends with Angelo Polizano who probably introduced him to his patrons the

[1] See *Archivio Storico Italiano.* Serie Terza. Tomo IX., Parte I., 1869; also *Florentia.* Isidoro del Lungo. Firenze, G. Barbèra, 1897.

Medici. The witty, clever, kind-hearted Matteo became indispensable to Lorenzo the Magnificent, with whom he was on such terms of intimacy as to write the following letter, rather a curious picture of the times as coming from a penniless young priest of twenty-seven to the ruler of Florence.

> "Lorenzo mine, have mercy. God well knows how and in what attitude I write to you. A chopping-board on my bed whereon lies my paper, my arm bare with upturned sleeve, I am as a dead man laden with bricks, with a head like a big onion on an arid mass of *cappelline*,[1] I seem to be all east wind. With trembling voice and hands I write, Signior mine, because the sacristan of Orto San Michele has just come to my bedside to tell me that the priest of my little church, which Your Magnificence promised me, is dead ; it is at Empoli and worth 12 or 15 florins a month, and there are no duties. . . . Now being vacant, Lorenzo, my life and hope, I throw myself into your arms. I know not what to say to you. I have nought but mine own mother-wit and my tongue. Do not judge, for the love of God, by my writing, but by my affection, my need, and the straits in which I find myself. I commend myself to you as heartily as I can, and will not again molest you. No more : in haste : I am sweating as though I were harnessed to a waggon. God keep you in health and prosperity, and inspire you to do what is best for the salvation of my soul."

[1] A very small kind of maccaroni.

The "little church at Empoli" was but a foretaste of many fatter livings which fell to Matteo Franco and which he sublet to others, as the Medici could not do without him. He taught all Lorenzo's children to read, and feelingly describes the trouble they gave him in one of his sonnets. Lorenzo speaks of him as "among the first and best-loved creatures of my house," and delighted in his witty conversation. Poliziano and Franco were as brothers, and his friendship with Piero and Bernardo Dovizi, of Bibbiena, both of them chancellors of the Medici, lasted till death parted them. From Piero, whom he calls "marrow of my heart," Matteo had no secrets, and poured out all his hopes, sorrows, and anxieties in long letters, when in later years he was repaying Lorenzo's affection tenfold by his devotion to his daughter Magdalena in Rome. A man who inspires ardent friendships generally makes bitter enemies, and our Matteo was no exception to the rule. Bernardo Bellincione and Luigi Pulci both hated him intensely, and the three poets abused each other in sonnets written in the choicest Tuscan to the amusement of all Florence. Bellincione dropped out of favour with the Medici, but Luigi Pulci, the friend and companion of childhood and youth, never lost his place in Lorenzo's heart. Indeed, until lately it was generally supposed that Franco and Pulci were in reality friends, and only wrote ferocious and biting sonnets to each other to amuse Lorenzo the Magnificent. But Sigr. Guglielmo Velpi conclusively proves, I think, that their animosity was very real, and that Matteo often had the best in this war of words.[1]

Even Lorenzo's austere and unlettered wife, Clarice Orsini, always ill at ease among her husband's brilliant friends, and at first suspicious of Matteo's biting tongue, soon discovered his many excellent qualities and never stirred from Florence without him. He became her treasurer, her almoner, and at length her attorney. A charming description is given in one of his letters of the meeting of mother and children on her return from the baths of Morba, near Volterra. Her boys rode out to meet her near San Casciano, and Matteo says:

> ". . . We met paradise full of young and festive angels, that is to say, Messers Giovanni Piero, Giuliano, and Gulio, together with their attendants. As soon as they saw their mother they threw themselves off their horses, some by themselves, others with the aid of their people, and they ran forward and cast themselves into the arms of Madonna Clarice with such joy and kisses and delight that a hundred letters would not describe it. Even I could not refrain from getting off my horse, and before they remounted I embraced them all twice; once for myself and once for Lorenzo. Darling little Giuliano said with a long O, O, O,

[1] *Giornale Storico della Letteratura Italiana*, vol. xvii., fasc. 50–51.

> 'Where is Lorenzo?' We answered, 'He has gone to Poggio to meet you.' Then he: 'Oh no, never,' almost in tears. You never beheld so touching a sight. He and Piero, who has become a beautiful boy, the finest thing, by God, you ever saw, somewhat grown, with a profile like an angel, and longer hair which stands out a little and is pretty to see. And Giuliano, red and fresh as a rose, smooth, clean and bright as a mirror, joyous, and with those contemplative eyes. Messer Giovanni also seems well, he has not much colour but is healthy and good-looking; and Gulio has a brown and wholesome skin [the two future Popes, Leo X. and Clement VII.] In short, all are as happy as can be. And thus, with great content and happiness, a joyous party we went by Via Maggio, Ponte a Santa Trinita, San Michele Berteldi, Santa Maria Maggiore, Canto alla Paglia, Via de Martegli, and entered into our house, *per infinita asecula aseculorum eselibera nos a malo amen. . . .*"

When Clarice, who was in very bad health, and therefore more uncertain in temper than usual, went to Rome in 1488 with her daughter Magdalena, who was affianced to the Pope's son, Francesco Cibo, Matteo accompanied her. Lorenzo was loth to part with his daughter, "more dear to him than one of his eyes," and wrote to his trusted old friend and ambassador at Rome, Messer Giovanni Lanfredini:

> "I much desire that Magdalena should return with her mother, for she is but a child, and the house of

Signor Francesco is badly governed, and also she will be a consolation to Clarice; but I wish this to be managed delicately so as to cause no displeasure to His Holiness or to Signor Francesco; I should receive it as a grace done to me, but whatever you arrange will be well done. . . . It seems to me that His Holiness in this and in other matters moves very slowly, and till now is chary of giving what little he has; for besides the well-being of Signor Francesco, I am distressed lest a daughter of mine should be in straits, and am almost in despair about this and the other matters, seeing the slowness, the variability, and the small attention bestowed on business there."

Piero de' Medici joined his mother in Rome, where he married Alfonsina Orsini, and the bride and bridegroom and Magdalena accompanied Clarice back to Florence. Matteo Franco remained behind, as Francesco Cibo had evidently discovered how active and honest he was, and had sent him to Stigliano, a half-ruined castle built on the site of an imperial villa, about thirty miles from Rome. The baths were once famous and had brought in a considerable income.

Matteo wrote a long and delightful letter, of which I give some extracts, from what he calls "this cess-pool of a bath," to his friend Ser Pietro Dovizi, Chancellor to Lorenzo the Magnificent:

"I cannot tell you how gracious and kind Madonna Clarice is to me, even saying two or three times that my

Lord [Francesco Cibo] had shown small discretion in taking me from her: 'See how I am left: I will not permit anyone but Franco to have the spending of my money, and I will eat nothing but what has passed through his hands; and then we never intended to give him Franco in order that he should bury him in a wood; he would do far better for himself, for Madonna Magdalena, and for his house, to keep him here.' This she repeated a hundred times. And twice she has sent for me since I have been at the baths, and kept me two or three days with her, until my Lord had to drive me back to Stigliano. They tell me that before going to Florence with Alfonsina, Magdalena made out a list of what she wanted to ask of my Lord for her journey; and on this list was, among other things:

"'A chaplain, and I wish for Franco.'

"'Then someone to write letters for me sometimes, and for that Franco will serve me well.'

"'And also your Lordship's necklace for the time I am in Florence.'

"'And such dresses, and such footmen, if it so pleases you, &c.' This list she gave in the evening to my Lord, and after he had read it he replied: 'I gladly give thee all, save only Franco and the necklace.' And the maiden said: 'Madonna Clarice desires above all things that he should come.' 'And I desire above all things that he should stay. They have nought to do with Franco once Lorenzo gave him to thee; and I wish him to be left here to see to thy interests, for the income of these baths I intend shall be for thee. Thou seest that I have no one here who does not rob me. He has done more good in the fifteen days he has been there than all my other people in the years that I have had the estate of Cervetri, &c.'

"All this was told me by my angel Mistress and Lady, who cried often about my coming here to stay, and I am told talks of me and wishes for me all day long; if it were not for this and for the recollection of Him in Florence, my soul and my heart, of whom I think in all my tribulations, so that, by the true God, Ser Piero, melancholy flies from me and my heart is so consoled that my soul is kept in my body. Otherwise I should have died a hundred times a day. . . .

"I have been at the baths of Stigliano since the 12th of March, and have already built bridges, churches, and hospitals, for there was nothing, and the baths I have arranged *alla Toscana*. . . . My room is disgusting—Bagno a Morba is a Careggi in comparison; accursed air, inhabitants like Turks, everything as bad as can be; day and night I fight with *bravi*, with soldiers, with swindlers, with venomous dogs, with lepers, with Jews, with madmen, with thieves, and with Romans. Now I go to the cook, now to the baker, then to the tavern, then to the clients in the inns; then I argue with the discontented and the sick at the hospital, then with the pedlar, then with the grocer, then with the chemist; then I go to the washerwoman, then to the grooms, then to the courier, then to the doctor, then to the priest. For I have brought all these people and all these things here; there were but bare walls and only half of those standing; in short, I have had to transport into this forest, from the smallest to the largest thing which may be needful for perhaps 10,000 people, who during these two months will visit these baths, so that every man may, for his money, have every convenience he may want. And I am alone to manage all this : during this month of May never a day has passed but there have been 100 or 150 persons ; rooms, beds, and the court-yard, are all full, and some days there have been over 300. Most of them stay three days and then go ; and I have to receive them all, to see to their food, to provide what they want and have not brought with them, grass, oats, hay, in short, everything ; for all they have to pay me, so I hope to glean over 400 ducats for Madonna Magdalena if God gives me health. I have here between cooks, innkeepers, bakers and others, about twenty-five men in my pay; and if you could see your Franco in this tempest and purgatory and whirl, host of this great inn of the devil, by God you would pity him. They comfort me by saying that Christ must wish me well if I escape without a beating, a knife in my ribs, a quarrel, or an illness, for no one has ever returned whole from here, God be praised for his mercies. Yet I am of good cheer, and have such faith in my fair dealing that I hope to do myself honour, if it pleases God. Till now I have pocketed about 100 ducats ; and all sorts and conditions of men have come. If I have not gained with the bad ones, I have not lost ; and most have gone away contented : from those of the better sort—courtiers, gentlemen, and the like—I think, I have gained affection and esteem, for since their return to Rome they have written to me and even sent me presents. Some day I hope to have some great joy, I

> would hope even in the—— of Lucifer the Great, serving for love of God, of Lorenzo and what is His."

In vain Lorenzo wrote to his Ambassador Lanfredini, at the end of May:

> "It would have been most pleasing to me as Signor Francesco is coming here [to Florence] that he should send Franco on before him to prepare his house, for I am alone, and so much occupied that I cannot attend to so many things. If Signor Francesco decides to send Franco let him come as soon as possible."

But Matteo remained in Rome, either still occupied at Stigliano, or kept by Pope Innocent VIII., who had named him his "commensale perpetuo" (*i.e.* free of his table), as the witty epigrams of Franco amused His Holiness, and did not, to his infinite regret, accompany Francesco Cibo to Florence. For the first time since the Pazzi conspiracy in 1478 the usual festivities for San Giovanni (June 24th) were again celebrated; the peasants flocked into the town to see the Pope's son, husband of the gentle Madonna Magdalena, and the crowd saluted him with cries of "Cibo e Palle."

Serdonati gives, in connection with this marriage, an interesting account of the sobriety of Lorenzo in private life and his magnificent treatment of strangers.

> "Francesco, on going to Florence to consummate his marriage, took many cavaliers and noble personages with

him, the flower of the Roman nobility. He was received with great splendour and lodged with all his people right royally. But soon Lorenzo, taking pleasure in seeing his son-in-law familiarly, or perchance thinking to gain yet more the benevolence of the Pope, invited him continually to dine at his house without ceremony, or as we say, 'alla casalinga.' Now it appears that the Florentines are generally held to be chary of spending their money, so he thought that those gentlemen who had accompanied him to honour his marriage, might be treated in like manner and was sorely troubled, fearing that afterwards in Rome the city of Florence and his relatives might be held up to ridicule; and fearing to hear what he would not wish, he dared not ask how they fared. But one day a Roman gentleman, who was intimate with him, saw how full of thought he was and asked the reason; and he answered that although he knew Lorenzo, his father-in-law, to be a man of great reputation and worth, yet he felt mortified because, on account of the usage of the city or for some other reason, his friends were treated in too homely a fashion; this pained him for them, but might be remedied by a speedy departure, and in Rome he would be there to indemnify them for whatever discomfort and annoyance they had undergone. Astonished at this speech, the cavalier replied that had the Pope himself been lodged as they were he could not have been more splendidly or magnificently entertained, cared for, served, and honoured, and that no one could desire more. So delighted was Francesco to hear this that he could not contain himself, and recounted all to his father-in-law, who with great urbanity replied that children, among whom he now reckoned Francesco, and strangers, and noble persons, such as accompanied him, were to be treated differently, the latter with all magnificence, partly for their own merits, partly out of respect for him and to do him honour; but that he had made no difference between him and his own children. This caused Francesco much satisfaction and pleasure, and greatly pleased the Pope when he heard of it, and all admired the wisdom and prudence of Lorenzo in all things public and private."[1]

On July 30th, 1488, Clarice died in the arms of her favourite daughter, Magdalena, who soon after went to live at Rome, when Matteo Franco became not only her chaplain and secretary, but her steward, cook, sick-nurse, and, at odd moments, poet. Many and long are the letters he writes about his "dear daughter." He analyses her frequent illnesses with the acumen of a skilled physician and the tenderness of a mother. Watching over her night and day, and hour by hour, only occasionally he lets us see how homesick he is, and how he longs to be once more in the palace in Via Larga with Lorenzo and his friends. Then, returning to his beloved patient, he recalls whose daughter she is, and shows his antipathy for her husband, and, indeed, for all "these Genoese," from the Pope downwards. Not that Francesco is

[1] *Vita e fatti d'Innocenzo VIII.* Scritta per m. Francesco Serdonati fiorentino ec. Milano; Ferrario, 1829. pp. 59-61.

unkind to his wife, but she loves him too much. He gambles all night, and Magdalena lies awake till dawn listening for his footstep. She ought to go out, breathe the fresh air, and take some exercise, and she longs in vain for her dear hills of Poggio and of Fiesole. She has become "as thin as a lizard," and Matteo's anxiety is shown in a very long and rather querulous letter to his constant correspondent, Ser Pietro Dovizi, the Chancellor, of which I give some extracts:

> "Ser Piero, you know for how long I have been telling you about the disorder of this house, and how day by day it increases, so that I am worn out; and how here a Florentine is as a Cross among devils, and also I have told you about the various maladies of Madonna. And as I doubt whether you read my letters through, I suspect all this will be new to you; for this doubt, and for my own satisfaction, and because I am bursting with anxiety and worry without knowing where to turn for counsel or help, and see such coldness and so little care and love for creatures much more important than Franco, that I take no thought about my own concerns, but cannot do the same about this. Never a man or a woman comes to this house, save perhaps once in a new moon, to know whether Madonna is alive or dead, let be that she has no sort of authority here; but just to know whether she is alive, for since our return she has always been shut up in the house, save for two days, when she went to Cervetri, and twice that she visited

His Holiness, and one evening that she supped at the bank. She is always ailing, and for her, poor child, no living soul seems to care. . . . Cursed be those cream cheeses, milk cheeses, pears, flasks of Trebbiano, bunches of fennel, and those medlars, which have never, never been sent to her by you or anyone else. These Genoese are splendidly housed and have every marvel of the world; but, not to speak of things of greater value, she, being the daughter of such a father and so good and charming, is not to be despised; yet the daughter of an exile would receive more attention than this poor patient child . . ."

and then, after many pages about her various ailments and the remedies used, and entreaties that Maestro Pier Leoni should be sent to visit her, he ends by urgent entreaties to be recalled, as he can bear such a life no longer.

But Matteo was still in Rome in 1492, when Magdalena's brother, Cardinal Giovanni de Medici, took up his abode there. A sad year it was for her, as Lorenzo the Magnificent died in April, her little girl soon afterwards, and her husband's father, the Pope, in July. Matteo Franco writes to his "Lord and most dear son Piero" a heartbroken letter on the death of his father:

"God be thy consolation, for nought else will serve. Consolation and comfort from any man alive will not suffice, and, even could it be of use, one who has lost all his own consolation and comfort is a bad consoler and comforter. . . . For 18 years I have eaten your bread and been nourished entirely by your house; soul, blood, flesh, and bones obey you more than myself, because they have received more from you than from me. . . ."

Innocent VIII., in spite of Magdalena's prayers, had never done anything for Matteo, so when a canonry of the cathedral of Florence fell vacant, she and Francesco wrote to Piero de Medici:

"Magnificent my brother Piero. From your ambassador and also from your most Revd. Cardinal, to whom I wrote as much as my sorrow would permit, you will have heard of our fresh tears, shed for our dead little girl. I will say no more, not to recall other deaths, and only pray God that this may be the last, and that he will console my afflicted Magdalena who cannot be comforted; so that her grief keeps me in constant fear, for her and for the child she carries in her bosom. God comfort and help us, and I pray of you when you write to comfort her, for there is much need of it. *Et de hoc satis.* It remains for me to say that you must be spokesman for Magdalena and for me with your Revd. Monsignore [Rinaldo Orsini, Archbishop of Florence, uncle of Piero and Magdalena] and induce him *ex corde* to grant what we have asked for a person belonging to us; and that is the canonry of Messer Carlo de' Medici for our and your slave and martyr Franco, who for love of us and of you is in Rome, aged, broken in health, and impoverished, to our great shame; one of the sorrows that Magdalena and I hold in our hearts is that we have never been able to do anything for him. For if you, Piero, knew as we do, how he has striven always for the honour and good of our house, and what he has done during the illnesses of Magdalena and of myself, more especially in this last one of our dead child, I know you to be not so ungrateful as to refuse to do much more for him than to obtain a canonry of XXX ducats. His Holiness and everyone, as I have written to Monsignore, who knows him here, are agreed. In short, persuade Monsignore to excuse himself with any man to whom he may have promised this canonry, even if it be a hundred times, by saying that he is more beholden to Magdalena (not to speak of myself) than to anyone. We ask for this canonry as a gift and a grace to ourselves. Tell his Grace that we insist on having it; and that could he see Magdalena in her bed begging with such heartfelt entreaties for this thing, and on the other side the martyr Franco, ill from the many discomforts he has suffered in our service, he would be ashamed to give us only so small a thing as this canonry. And now, having also written to his Grace *ad longum*, I will add no more, only recapitulating to you that at any cost we must have this canonry; if not for the obligations you are under to Franco, for ours, which we know better than anyone.

"Magdalena and I send greetings to you all, and pray you may be kept in health, and above all our Innocent wishes to be remembered to you. Romae, last day of May, MCCCCLXXXXII.

"FRATER FRANC. CIBO.

"From my heart and with my own hand I adjure you, brother dear, to cause Monsignore to bestow this canonry on us; because I want it at all costs, and I think I deserve it.

"Soror Magdalena Cibo de Medici (*manu propria*)."

On June 23rd the canons of the cathedral of Florence assembled in chapter "receperunt in canonicum dominum Mathæum Franchi"; and Angelo Poliziano wrote to Piero de' Medici to express his delight at having his old friend as a colleague. His elegant Latin epistle gives a pleasant picture of Magdalena's "slave and martyr."

"Let me thank thee, O my Piero, for having exerted authority and trouble to get Ser Matteo Franco made one of our canons. Thou knowest how great a friend he is to me, a man, of a truth, worthy of this and of any other honour, in despite of certain jealous persons. He gained the good graces of thy most learned father by his pleasant and urbane accomplishments, writing those Burchielesque poems in the vulgar tongue, which are to-day praised all over Italy. Well do I remember that thy father taught thee, as a small child, just for fun, some of the most facetious of these rhymes; and in conversation thou wouldst lisp them, ornamenting them with thy infantile graces and affectations. Of a truth the conversation and society of Franco is no less agreeable; for proverbs, stories, and curious knowledge he is worth untold gold, acute yet discreet, as becomes one who is neither scurrilous nor licentious, who is never tiresome, but always speaks to the point, never talking at random or without reflection. Thy father, Lorenzo, therefore always took him with him in his *villegiature* and when he went to any baths, as being so pleasant a companion. And when Magdalena, thy sister, married and settled at Rome he placed him with her as counsellor, so that she, being an unexpert girl who had never quitted her mother's side, should have a friend by her in case of need. Customs were new and strange there, but Franco, at once quick and patient, gained universal esteem, and to Magdalena it was as though she had all the comfort of her paternal home. I hear he is a great favourite with His Holiness and with several cardinals, and that the administrators of thy bank are devoted to him. In so short a time he has even mastered the intricacies of law and of the Roman courts, so that he is now looked up to as an authority. He is, in short, our Franco, one of those versatile spirits who are themselves at home everywhere and with every-one. But where he is a master is in domestic economy, knowing not only how to tell the servants what to do but how to do it. I must add another singular virtue of his: in making friends and keeping them when made, he has no rival. The affection between us is well known and we pass, thank God, for a rare couple of friends. So much so, that it seems to me that thou hast made me canon a second time, by adding him, my second self, to our chapter; and in his person I seem to receive no less honour than I did in mine own."

Matteo accompanied Piero de' Medici as chaplain

to Rome, when he went to do homage to Pope Alexander VI. after the death of Innocent VIII., chosen, no doubt, for his intimate knowledge of the intrigues at the Roman Court. Soon after his return he was named "spedalingo," *i.e.* rector and head of the hospital at Pisa, probably because his "dear heart" Magdalena, and her husband, Francesco Cibo, had taken up their residence there. In August, 1494, Giovanni Cambi, writing to Piero about Pisan matters, adds, "but I must not forget to give you news of Franco, he has so many sick that all the beds are full." This is the last mention of the genial, kindly, witty priest, who died on September 6th, a victim, probably, to one of the epidemics so frequent in olden times.

Two Florentine Hospitals

THE HOSPITAL OF THE INNOCENTI

Many of my readers have doubtless admired Andrea della Robbia's charming swaddled babies on the front of the "Innocenti" hospital in Florence, who look down so appealingly with outstretched hands on all passers-by. But to Milan belongs the honour of first inaugurating a hospital for illegitimate children—innocents, as they are called in Italy. A priest, Dateo, in 787, "moved to compassion by the number of poor new-born babes who were thrown into the drains, or into the river, to hide their mothers' shame, without being baptised," founded it, and kept the children until they were seven; at which age they were "*liberi et absoluti ab omni vinculo servitutis*, thus saving, not only their lives, but also their legal status, making men of them and not chattels." Florence followed suit later, when in 1218 a rich and much-esteemed citizen, Guidalotto di Volto dall' Orco, one of the captains of Santa Maria instituted by Fra Piero da Verona to combat the heresy of the Paterins, built, and gave to the Church, the hospital of Santa Maria a San Gallo outside the walls, with which an older hospital, mentioned in the *Liber censum Romanæ Ecclesiæ* in 1192, seems to have been incorporated. In 1294 a general Council of the People decided to place the hospital under the patronage of the great Guild of Silk Merchants, and privileges were bestowed on it by many popes. Amongst others Innocent IV. allowed mass to be said in a low voice when the city was under interdict—provided the chapel door was closed and no bell was rung. The old registers tell us that to every child put out to nurse was given linen, three pieces of flannel, a fur-lined cloak for winter, and a cradle; and when weaned they were taken back into the hospital. Occasionally a pious citizen would adopt one of the children "for the love of God," promising, in the case of a boy, to teach him a handicraft; if a girl, to find her a husband and to give her a dowry.

In 1421 the Guild of Silk Merchants of Por Santa Maria began building the actual "Hospital of the Innocents" in Piazza dei Servi, and the Signoria named the Guild "inventor, founder and master of the said hospital with full powers to elect the governor and other officials, granting at the same time such privileges and exemptions as were enjoyed by the hospital of Santa Maria Nuova." Filippo Brunelleschi was the architect employed, and his pupil Francesco della Luna directed the works; but, probably for want of funds, the building was only finished in 1445, when the Consuls of the Guild invited the commune and the people of Florence to be present at the ceremony of inauguration on the 24th January. The Patriarch of Jerusalem was then Papal Legate in Florence, and he accompanied the Bishop of Fiesole in solemn procession from the Duomo, followed by the Consuls of the Guild and much people. But the church was only consecrated six years later by St. Antonino, the pious Archbishop of Florence, who placed under the altar stone a leaden box containing relics, which was found when the church was repaired in 1615. It was with a feeling of reverence that I took up the little box, still containing the relics enveloped in discoloured cotton wool, which had been touched by the hands of the saintly Archbishop. On the lid is inscribed:

> "FR. ANTONIUS . DE . FLORĒ
> TIA: ORD. P̄DICATORUM
> ARCHIEP̄US . FLORĒTINUS
> CŌSECRAVIT ECCLEIĀ
> A.D. MCCCCLI. D. XI. APRELIS."

On one side is engraved "UNIVERSITA PORTAE S . M . ECCLESIAM ET HOSPITALE FACIENDUM CURAVIT," on the other "RELIQUIE SANCTORUM EUGENII CRESCETII ET ADOSĒ."[1] On one end is the barred door of the Guild of Silk Merchants, with the words "ARS PORTAE S . C . E . M." and on the other a baby lying on a cup,

[1] Meaning: Abdon and St. Senen. Persians who were cruelly martyred at Rome A.D. 250. See J. P. Migne. *Dictionnaire hagiographique*, tome i., 1850.

probably the first arms of the hospital before the swaddled upright baby was adopted, known all the world over by the exquisite *tondi* on the front of Brunelleschi's *loggia*,[1] with the inscription "S. HOSPITALIS INNOCENTIUM."

The number of "innocents" increased so rapidly that in 1448 the Guild of Silk Merchants decreed that one soldo in every lira paid for winding silk, and two soldi in every lira paid for weaving damask, should be set aside, after one-third of the total sum had been deducted for the Congregation of Weavers, for the benefit of the hospital. At the same time the Signoria ordered that all merchandise of whatsoever description, saving wheat and building materials, should pay one soldo for every horse, mule, or donkey-load, brought into the town, to the hospital, and exempted it from the tax on salt and on eatables. Some years later this tax was commuted for a certain yearly payment by the city, and this still continues, in spite of an attempt by the commune in 1872 to obtain a decree cancelling the ancient law.

Still the "family," as the old records call it, grew so rapidly, that in 1463 the hospital of San Gallo was incorporated with the new Foundling Hospital in

[1] "Of the fourteen medallions which now decorate it, only ten are by Andrea, the other two at either end having been added by the Ginori Fabbrica in recent times."

See Maud Cruttwell. *Luca and Andrea della Robbia and their Successors.* J. M. Dent and Co., London, 1902.

order to increase its revenues; and three years later the Consuls of the Guild petitioned the Signoria to remit certain arrears of taxes on house property, saying "if ever this hospital was in need of help, it is so now, with 700 mouths to feed: 400 of them being out at nurse, and fifty being girls of a marriageable age." In a later petition we find that the number of children was so large, and the debts were so pressing, that the wet-nurses could not be paid, and some of the babies died of hunger, "a thing that cannot be tolerated by men of gentle and kindly nature, as are the Florentines, or heard tell of without horror and tears." In 1513 the number of "mouths" had increased to 1,320, when Leo X. bestowed spiritual privileges on anyone who maintained a foundling for one year, and many of the great Florentine families made handsome donations.

When Cosimo I. became Grand Duke, he ordered that the Governor, or as he was then called the Prior, should be elected for life, and not only live in the hospital, but have his meals with the other officials, a rule that was only abolished in 1742. An edict was also passed that the hospital should have a soldi in the lira out of every fine, three golden florins for every sentence of death, and one for all amputations or bodily punishments, but if the sentence was remitted, the claims of the hospital were to be satisfied before the remission took effect.

The small remuneration given to the wet-nurses made it difficult to place out the "innocents," so that many died, and it was not until the Grand Duke Francesco, in 1577, told the Prior that in Spain cow's milk was often given to children, that "the doctors consulted together and a cow was bought, whose milk was given to the babies in certain glasses with nozzles, and it suited them well," This is the first record of bringing up children by hand in the city of Florence.

The first experiment of inoculating smallpox in Florence was also made in the Innocenti hospital in 1756 with good results, but it does not appear to have found much favour with the public in general. The Prior must have had enough to do, as the family numbered 3,855; but many children, instead of being taken back into the hospital, were left with their foster-mothers for a very small annual payment, and brought up as peasants. In 1801 vaccination was attempted by the doctor of the Innocenti, but he failed; probably the vaccine, which came from Vienna, was too old. Four years later a Dr. Sacco obtained the permission of the Queen Regent Maria Luisa to vaccinate some of the "innocents," whom he afterwards inoculated with smallpox, without any ill effects. Maria Luisa then ordered that all over Tuscany foundlings were to be vaccinated.

In Florence the surnames "Innocenti," "Degl'

Innocenti," "Nocentini," are often met with, as until the beginning of the last century the children only received a Christian name when they were baptised, and the name of "Innocent" was often added to distinguish them. The Grand Duke Ferdinand III. then ordered that to every child should be given a surname in order to remove the slur of illegitimacy. In 1903 the "family" belonging to the hospital numbered 4,949, including the sisters, nurses, servants, etc., so the office of Governor is no sinecure.

The Virgin of the Annunciation in the courtyard of the hospital by Andrea della Robbia has a dignity which recalls the works of Luca, and the frame of smiling cherubs' heads is charming,[1] and in the little old-world gallery is a stately Madonna and Child, which once was in the church; it is probably one of Luca della Robbia's earliest works, as the modelling of the Virgin's right arm is faulty, and the Child seems to weigh heavy on her.[2] There is also a fine painted terra-cotta bust of Messer Cione Pollini, a grave, severe man, with the Florentine turban headdress. He is erroneously styled the founder of the hospital; what he did was to cede all his rights over the hospital of Santa Maria della Scala, in 1536, and allow it to be incorporated with the Innocenti, to the great advantage of its finances. A glowing picture by

[1] *Opus cit.*, p 186. [2] *Opus cit.*, p. 121.

Pier di Cosimo, the Madonna with the Infant Christ giving the ring to S. Catherine, while old women kneel and offer Him flowers and SS. Peter and Mark with angels stand behind, is fine. The end of the room is taken up by a fresco by Poccetti (1610) depicting the murder of the Innocents; but in the background on the right hand are the servants of the hospital preparing food, and masters giving lessons to the children, and Cosimo II. in front paying a visit to the hospital, received by little children kneeling.

THE HOSPITAL OF SANTA MARIA NUOVA

ONE side of the Piazza Santa Maria Nuova is occupied by the fine *loggia* of the hospital designed by Buontalenti, with its walls decorated by frescoes; some of which, done by Pomarancio, are so bad that the saying in Florence is that the sick are inside the walls while the deformed are outside. But those on either side of the door of S. Egidio, which forms an integral part of the hospital, are interesting and curious as studies of costume. One represents the Spedalingo, or Governor, Michele da Panzano, who began the new church "in September, 1418, taking counsel with his friend Lorenzo di Bicci," writes Vasari, on the site of the ancient and far smaller one. In one Michele is kneeling before Pope Martin V., who consecrated the church in 1420; in the other he is kissing the hand of Martin, who gives him a brief, and the officials of the hospital are standing round. These frescoes were painted in 1424 by Bicci di Lorenzo, son of the architect of the church, and he also made the terra-cotta Coronation of the Virgin above the portal. In the choir of the church is a fine, but rather cold Madonna and Child by Andrea della Robbia, probably one of his latest works,[1] and an ambry by Mino da Fiesole, chiefly remarkable for its exquisite little door by Lorenzo Ghiberti. To the right of the entrance is a plain tomb where the founder of the hospital, Folco di Ricovero de' Portinari, is believed to have been buried. Wherever Dante is read and loved, Folco de' Portinari is known as the father of Beatrice, whose name calls up before us an image of radiant loveliness, for does not the poet tell us—

> ". . . Whatsoever bait
> Of art or nature in the human flesh,
> Or in its limit'd resemblance can combine
> Through greedy eyes to take the soul withal,
> Were to her beauty nothing. . . ."

After fighting in the ranks of the Imperial troops and sharing the exile of the great Ghibelline families, Folco returned to Florence in 1280, and at once took a high place in the government of the city. Charitable and kindly, his heart was touched by the suffering of the poor, and he determined to build

[1] See *Luca and Andrea della Robbia*, etc., by Maud Cruttwell. J. M. Dent and Co., 1902.

a hospital outside the second circuit of the walls of Florence, near the Porta degli Albertinelli, where he possessed houses and land. Tradition says that the first idea was given by Tessa, an old servant of the family, who devoted herself to nursing the sick in a small house belonging to her master. The effigy of an old woman in the dress of a nun of the Order of the Oblates, holding a book on which a crutch is worked, the arms of the hospital, and with an inscription underneath of the seventeenth century stating that it represents Monna Tessa who induced Folco to found the hospital, is pointed out in the entrance as a confirmation of the story. It originally stood in the chapel of S. Elisabeth in the church of S. Egidio, and Richa, in his history of the Florentine churches, gives an inscription which vanished when the old altar was swept away during the restoration of the hospital and the church some two hundred years ago. Passerini suggests that this may have given rise to the legend of the charitable maid-servant.[1] The inscription, in rude Gothic characters, ran—

> "Pro anima di Monna Tessa
> Fatt' e questo per dir la messa
> Mogle fu di Turi bastaio
> Edi pago (?) ogni danaro
> Mille trecento e vensette
> Di 4 luglio del secol partette."

[1] *Storia degli Stabilimenti di Beneficenza*, L. Passerini. Firenze, Le Mounier, 1858.

In 1288 the hospital was opened with twelve beds, and Folco de' Portinari—"he who had been the father of so great a miracle as this most noble Beatrice was seen to be"—died the following year, reserving by his will the patronage to his descendants. Not many years passed before it had to be enlarged, and an old chronicler notes that when Messer Benedetto da Montebonello, the Governor, began building in 1312, "an exceeding great and brilliant comet appeared in the heavens above Santa Maria Nuova, at which the citizens rejoiced as being of good augury for the future of the good work." The orchard of the friars of S. Egidio was turned into a cemetery, which must have been a ghastly sight, as we read that "the walls were adorned with bones arranged in patterns, while here and there stood a whole skeleton in a niche, with an appropriate motto. After Martin V. consecrated the new church in 1420 many noble people elected to die in the hospital, as the Pope, when kneeling at the entrance to the cemetery, had gathered up a handful of earth, conceding to all who died within the walls of Santa Maria Nuova as many years of indulgence as he held grains of earth in his hand."

Old Matteo Villani, writing in 1348, when the plague decimated Florence, says: "The hospital is most charitable and is full of sick, both men and women, who are nursed with much care; there is abundance of good things for the sustenance of the sick, and it is governed by men and women of saintly and charitable lives."

Cristoforo Landini, more than a century later, also bears witness to the good management of Santa Maria Nuova. "Herein, one month with another, more than 300 sick are nursed. The beds are ever, although it is a difficult matter, kept white and clean, and there are always watchers of the sick, who minister to their wants. Neither food nor medicine are of a common order, but adapted to each patient according to his malady. Doctors, physicians, and surgeons are always ready, who prescribe for every case. Therefore many strangers, both nobles and rich men, being oppressed with sickness whilst travelling, have elected to be nursed there."

People were satisfied with little in those days, for as there were only 150 beds in the men's wards, and eighty in the women's, two or three sick persons were often put into one bed. Still the fame of the admirable management spread abroad. Leo X. sent his body physician to study the rules and regulations, and our King Henry VIII. asked Francesco de' Portinari to send him a copy, as he desired to found a similar institution in London. The long and curious document, written in rather grandiloquent Latin, is published by Passerini.[1]

During the death struggle between the Republic

[1] *Op. cit.* in Appendix.

and the Pope and Emperor, the hospital was ruined, and the state of its finances only began to improve under the reign of the Grand Duke Cosimo I. Ferdinando I. ordered that a nominee of his own should superintend the working of the hospital, and named four Senators, deputed to report to him at stated intervals. The first thing they proposed was to free the hospital from the tyranny of the Padri Crociferi, the Crutched Friars, attached to the church of S. Egidio, or S. Giles, the patron saint of cripples; hence was, I suppose, derived the arms of the hospital, a crutch. These friars had gradually assumed the lay, as well as the spiritual, direction, and the struggle was a fierce one, they being supported by the Archbishop of Florence and the Roman Curia, as well as by an ancient diploma of the Portinari. Cosimo II., to avoid all future interference in the management, induced the Portinari to cede all their rights in 1617, against a commenda of 10,000 scudi in the Order of S. Stefano, and the friars were turned out "to the great consolation of the governor." Additional wards were built, but proved insufficient, and the poor complained bitterly that when taken to the hospital to be cured of one malady they often caught a worse by being put into the same bed with other patients. So in 1650 Monsignore Ricasoli, the Governor, determined to build a new wing for male patients, and when opened "the citizens saw with wonder and admiration the new iron bedsteads for one person only." Ten years later another large ward was built over the cemetery, which was moved behind the church between two wings of the hospital, and at the same time the underground passage, which connects the convent of the Oblate nuns with the hospital, and is marked by square holes, covered with thick iron bars, in the Piazza, was opened.

In 1742 three doctors, among them Antonio Cocchi, the friend of Horace Walpole and of Horace Mann, described by the Earl of Cork as "a man of most extensive learning," were charged to examine into the condition of the hospital and report to the Council of Regency. Five hundred sick were then under treatment; the food is described as bad in quality and insufficient in quantity, and the medical assistance as wretched. Little or nothing was done, and twenty years later another commission was appointed who made the same complaints, adding, that in consequence of the decadence of the silk and wool industries in Florence, the misery among artisans was so great that, after begging in the streets all day, they stole into the hospital at night and took possession of any empty beds, pretending to be sick in order to get a night's rest, and perhaps a little food, before they were turned out the following morning. Cocchi also strongly remonstrated against the danger arising from the burial of so many corpses in the centre of the building. "The exhalations are pestilential, and so dense that if a person goes there at night with a light the very air takes fire." Francis of Lorraine, Emperor of Austria and Grand Duke of Tuscany, subscribed 4,000 scudi, and his example being followed by others, the cemetery was removed. During alterations made a few years ago, I was told that three feet below the surface of the soil the men came upon a layer of bones nine feet thick. The Grand Duke Pietro Leopoldo also gave large sums out of his privy purse, and named the Senator Marco Covoni Commissary-in-Chief of Santa Maria Nuova, who drew up most excellent rules and regulations and saw that they were carried out. The adjoining convent, Degli Angioli, was incorporated with the hospital, and a fine but scarified and repainted Crucifixion, painted by Andrea di Castagno, is still to be seen in one of the cloisters. In another, the first from the entrance, is a poor Deposition of the Della Robbia school, and above a door near by stands a curious and majestic painted stucco of the fourteenth century—a Madonna and Child with two angels drawing aside curtains, evidently by some North Italian master.

The magnificent triptych by Hugo van der Goes, now in the Uffizi Gallery, was painted in 1470 for Tommaso Portinari, head of the Medici bank at Bruges, as an offering to the church of the hospital founded by his ancestor Folco at Florence. He is kneeling with his two young sons in the left wing of the picture, and his wife and daughter, named Beatrice, are opposite. It hung on the left of the high altar in S. Egidio, until all the pictures belonging to the hospital were collected in a room in the convent of the Oblate nuns, opposite the hospital. The whole collection, among them two Hans Hemlings, was taken over some years ago by the Italian Government for an absurdly small sum, about one fourth what the van der Goes alone was worth.

A September Day in the Valley of the Arno

Leaving Florence by the Porta S. Frediano we drove about four miles to the ancient Badia a Settimo, famous in the political as well as the religious annals of Tuscany. The peasants were as busy as bees, preparing casks and vats for the vintage, and the universal hammering was quite deafening, mingled with the beating out of the *sagina*—a kind of millet much grown for making brooms, which are sent by shiploads to England and America. Most beautiful are the fields of the tall *sagina;* the light green leaves bend gracefully to the breeze, and the loose head of seed falls like a cascade of chestnut-coloured rain from the tops of the slender stems. To English eyes the wealth of grapes appeared incredible, and the colours marvellous. From maple to maple hung long garlands of vines in fantastic shapes, *Buon Amico*, or "good friend," with large loose bunches of purple-black grapes, *Trebbiano*, brilliant yellow, with the sunny side stained a deep brown, *Uva Grassa*, a dull yellow-green, and the lovely *Occhio di Pernice*, or "partridge's eye," of a light pink with ruby lines meandering about in every grape, the flavour of which was quite equal to its beauty. The *contadini* were much amused at our admiration, and insisted on our tasting the various kinds of grapes. Immense golden pumpkins, melons, water-melons, and scarlet tomatoes were being picked, and on some of the farms the women and children were busily employed in making round cakes of the latter fruit, and drying them in the sun for winter consumption. Outside the windows hung branches of the *Acacia horrida*, of which the crown of thorns is said to have been made; each long thorn bore a crop of skinned figs, the gelatinous, sweet drops of juice oozing out and congealing in the sun's rays. On the low walls surrounding the threshing-floors were flat baskets, boards, and plates, covered with split peaches and figs drying in the sun, for the children to eat in winter with their bread.

About half-way we crossed the Greve by a picturesque old bridge, with a pretty little oratory perched on the top. It was built by Pisan prisoners in the days when every Italian city was at deadly feud with its neighbour.

Turning off the high-road to the right, the gate-tower of the Badia a Settimo rose high above the plain, and soon the long, picturesque line of machicolated walls of what is left of the monastery came into sight. In 940 it was a dependency of the powerful Counts of Borgonuovo, or Fucecchio. Count Lotario enlarged the abbey, which was inhabited by the Cluniacense monks, in 1004. His son, Count Gugliemo Bulgaro, was a munificent patron, and among other possessions gave them the church of San Salvatore, in the Apennines, with the vast territory of Stale (hospice), as a hermitage for those monks who desired to retire from the world. Stale in after times was raised to a countship, and in the fourteenth century was an apple of discord between Bologna and Florence. Count Gugliemo was a friend of St. John Gualberto, and asked him to reform the monastery of Settimo, where abuses and evil customs of all sorts had taken root; and until his death, in 1073, the saintly abbot of Vallombrosa reigned supreme, and introduced his own rule. It was here by his order that St. Peter Igneus, in 1068, went through the ordeal of fire, in the presence of an immense concourse of people. The following inscriptions still exist attesting the fact:

> "Igneus hic Petrus medios pertransiit ignes,
> Flammarum victor, sed magis haereseos."

> "Hoc in loco, miraculo S. Joannis Gualberti, quidam fuere confutati Haeretici. MLXX."

Several of the Laurentian codexes were executed about this time in the Badia a Settimo, which were afterwards bought by the Medici for a large sum for their library in Florence: the monks were also famous agriculturists and hydraulic engineers.

Emperors and popes took the abbey under their protection, and in 1236 Gregory IX. gave it to the Cistercians, and took it under the immediate protection of the Holy See. The exemplary life of the new inhabitants of the monastery so gained the esteem of the public that the Signory of Florence confided to them the administration of the taxes, the maintenance of the city walls and the bridges, the construction of the castles and fortified places in the Florentine district, and finally declared them keepers of the great seal. The large possessions of the abbey served as a guarantee, and the monks were exempt from all taxes to the state. How considerable their revenue must have been is proved by the large sum each abbot paid on investiture to the Court of Rome—a thousand golden florins. Various mills were erected by them on the banks of the Arno; but the weirs and locks interfered with navigation, and caused such serious inundations that, in 1385, the Republic of Florence ordered their demolition.

The abbey suffered so much during the siege of Florence in 1529 that Paul IV. permitted the abbot and the greater part of his monks to migrate to the monastery of Cestello, near Porta Pinti, which had belonged to them since 1442. Tradition assigns the campanile of the Badia, a hundred and eleven feet high, a model of elegance, to the munificent Count Gugliemo. At the base it is round, about half-way up it becomes hexagonal, with small machicolations at the summit, and a pyramidical roof. Vasari, in his life of Niccolò Pisano, attributes this lovely bell-tower to the famous Pisan architect, who was certainly consulted about alterations to the church, and, in fact, it resembles the well-known campanile of San Niccolò at Pisa.

On approaching the Badia a Settimo, the tall gate-tower is most imposing, with its machicolations and the curious large alto-relievo of our Lord and two saints, built in brick and mortar, and evidently of great antiquity. There are still traces of painted angels' heads in the niche containing the figures. Below the feet of Christ is a stone, bearing the lily of Florence and an illegible inscription; under that again is a marble slab with "Anno Domini MCCXXXVI S. S. Dmn. N. Gregorius IX. dedit hoc Monasterium de Septimo Ordin. Cisterc. cum esset liberum et exemptum ab omni regio patronatu, quod in plena libertate a dicto Ordine pacifice possidetur."

This tower in old times was connected with the fortress-like walls with which the Republic of Florence surrounded the monastery after the inroads of the Pisans under Giovanni Acuto (Sir John Hawkwood), in 1371. There were three other towers, and a broad walk all round the top of the walls, which were defended by a moat, and each tower had a drawbridge. How imposing the Badia must have been in those days, before the Arno had deposited over fifteen feet of mud, which conceals so much of the ancient structure! · Now the monastery is a private villa, and the cloisters, with their slender columns and beautifully carved capitals, resound to the pitter-patter of children's feet and the joyous laughter of young girls. The refectory of the monks, more than half buried, has been divided into cellars, and the fine old abbey church, with its solemn, antediluvian-looking columns, is the *tinaia* where the wine is made. Huge vats are ranged round the walls, and the lithe, brown-limbed *contadini* tread the foaming must, and sing their gay *stornelli*, where the black-robed monks once chanted hymns and psalms. One can judge of the original height of the building by one column which is excavated to its base, and of which there is much less above, than under ground.

The present church was built in the thirteenth century at right angles to the ancient edifice, and nearer the campanile. Round the choir runs a pretty frieze of the school of Luca della Robbia, four-winged angels' heads alternating with the kneeling lamb holding a banner, emblem of the guild of wool manufacturers. The high altar is a magnificent specimen of *pietra dura* work, and Giovanni di San Giovanni used his facile brush in 1629 to great effect in the left-hand chapel, where is a small marble ambry, or receptacle for the holy oil, by Desiderio da Settignano—a perfect jewel. Above the altar of this chapel, behind painted doors, stands a large silver casket containing the bones of St. Quentin, whose story was related in a most graphic manner by the priest's nephew, a small boy of about thirteen. He demurred to showing us the reliquary, as it entailed fetching two keys and lighting all the candles; but he informed us that St. Quentin was beheaded in Paris a thousand years ago. By a miracle his body was transported to a church on the opposite side of the Arno, which, however, the saint did not like, so the silver chest floated across the river, and in 1187 was brought to the Badia a Settimo, and deposited in the centre of the church in front of the high altar. "Ma non ci volle stare, pover uomo" (but he would not remain there, poor fellow), continued our informant, "and every morning the monks found him in this chapel, and so here he is, but without his head, for he could not find it when he left Paris. However, the box is full of bones," and the boy moved his two arms up and down as though violently shaking in imagination the remains of the poor saint, to make them rattle. As the present church, with St. Quentin's chapel, dates several hundred years later than the finding of the silver casket, we may be allowed to place a note of interrogation against the powers of migration of the headless saint.

To the right of the high altar is the ancient Spini

chapel, which must have been detached from the original church, as is the Cappella degli Spagnuoli in Sta. Maria Novella at Florence, and been entered from the cloisters. There are still dim traces of frescoes said to be by Buffalmacco. Now the chapel is like a cavern, as the deposit of the river has raised the surface of the ground to such a degree that the spring of the arches nearly touches the floor. There is an inscription setting forth that this chapel was built for the soul of Lapi des Spinis, in 1315.

High banks and dykes now keep the Arno in some control, but the tremendous flood of 1844 filled the chapel to the roof with muddy water, and completed the ruin of three or four fine pictures which were in the sacristy. The peasants near by had to take their bullocks and horses up into the bedrooms to save them from drowning; it seems that the poor beasts went upstairs willingly enough, "but all the king's horses and all the king's men" could not get them down again, so that in some instances the oxen had to be slaughtered and carried down piecemeal.

We were informed by the priest that when the present church was built it stood high above the level of the ground, and was approached by a flight of steps, now buried. The bases of the pillars which support the *loggia* in front of the church are more than half covered, and the tombs which were let into the walls have disappeared. The cenotaph of the

Countess Gasdia, wife of the great Count Gugliemo Bulgaro, is still to be seen, with an inscription above it recording the burial of her daughter-in-law, the Countess Cilla, who died in 1096. It must have been placed in its present position when the ancient abbey-church was abandoned.

Passing through the village of San Colombano, we drove along pretty country lanes, the hedges aglow with the scarlet berries of the orange thorn, and the trees clothed in vines, towards Lastra a Signa. At one farm they had begun the vintage; men, women, and children were busily occupied, the men on ladders cut down the *pendice* (two vine canes twisted carefully together in the early spring, with the eyes turned outwards), while the women picked off the leaves, which serve as fodder for the cattle. The finest *pendice* are hung up inside the *loggia* which almost invariably adorns a Tuscan farmhouse, in order to dry the grapes gradually for colouring and strengthening the wine after the first fermentation. The stately white oxen were chewing the cud, and the red ox-cart with a large vat tied on, and the wooden *bigoncia*, all stained with the red vine juice, looked most Bacchanalian. A handsome young *contadino* came along at a swinging pace with a *bigoncia* poised on one shoulder, in which purple and yellow grapes were piled high, and emptied the contents with a thud and a splash into the vat, which, when full, went slowly home to the *tinaia*, where the grapes were transferred to the larger vats after being well crushed.

The mediæval machicolated walls and towers and the old gateways of Lastra a Signa are intact. A fortified castle, called Gangalandi, was erected in 1226 to defend the road to Pisa (after the destruction of the ancient fortress of Monte Orlando in 1107), which was taken and burnt by the Pisans, aided by their English auxiliaries, in 1364. With proverbial astuteness the Florentines contrived some years later to bribe Giovanni Acuto (Sir John Hawkwood), the famous *condottiere*, to leave his Pisan masters and enter their service. His portrait, on his war-horse, is over the right-hand door of the cathedral of Florence, painted by Paolo Uccello in *terra verde*, in 1436. The action of the horse of the "Incliti Militis Domini Joannis Aguti" has given rise to endless discussion among mathematicians and philosophers of the Renaissance, which are amusing enough. He is evidently ambling, so that Paolo Uccello is unjustly called *pictor ineptus* by one of these learned scholars for making the horse raise the two off-legs simultaneously.

By his advice the Republic of Florence rebuilt Lastra a Signa in 1377, and twenty years later the unfortunate little town was invested and taken by Alberigo, captain of Galeazzo Visconti, Lord of

LASTRA A SIGNA

Face page 76

Milan, who was at deadly feud with the Signory. Again the walls were restored; and in 1529, when the Imperialists besieged Florence, Francesco Ferrucci, whose headquarters were at Empoli, five miles down the river, garrisoned Lastra a Signa with some of his bravest troops. The Prince of Orange sent a strong force of Spaniards with scaling-ladders to take the place, who were repulsed with considerable loss; but munitions ran short in the fortress, and while negotiations were going on, five hundred more Spanish lances arrived with battering-rams, effected an entrance on the south-east side, and cut the gallant defenders to pieces.

There is nothing remarkable in the village, save a picturesque *loggia*, still bearing traces of lavish decoration, which was part of the hospital for pilgrims once existing inside the walls. It has been barbarously maltreated; part is now a theatre, the rest is carpenters' shops. The population is squalid and miserable enough, and do not bear a good name; they are mostly employed in plaiting, sewing, and ironing straw hats, and the clatter of the hopper used for sorting the straw is incessant. The so-called Leghorn hats are all plaited in the lower Val d'Arno, and before the introduction of the cheap Japanese reed hats the women earned so much that the men did not think it worth while to work, and spent their time in gambling and loitering. Straw hats have diminished so much in price that a woman barely earns twopence a day, unless she is very expert, and can do the finest plait with fifteen or more straws, or is clever enough to invent a new pattern.

Skirting the fine walls we turned to the left, opposite the Portone del Baccio, the southern gate-tower of Lastra a Signa, now used as a prison, and followed the old Pisan road, up the valley of Rimaggio, to see the castle of Malmantile, some two and a half miles hence. The monastery of St. Lucia crowns the hill on our right, built where once stood the fortress of Monte Orlando, and in the quiet convent garden under the solemn cypresses are still some fragments of the ancient walls of the castle, the last stronghold of the great Counts of Fucecchio in this neighbourhood, destroyed by the Florentines in 1107.

The road to Malmantile by the little stream of Rimaggio is beautiful. The steep hillsides clothed with heather and pines, the cyclamen and the autumn crocus, or colchicum, glowing in the sunlight, the last year's leaves of the Christmas roses, yellow, bright brown, and black, and the shaggy goats climbing among the jutting rocks, formed a picture worthy of the brush of Salvator Rosa.

We passed four water-mills, and then, perched on a well-wooded knoll, with jagged rocks and a tangled undergrowth of honeysuckle, heather and brambles, saw the farmhouse of St. Antonio, which must in old times have been a fortress, dominating the valley. It is picturesque enough, all corners, angles, and arches, with a grey tower, now the home of numerous pigeons—

> "Cooing all their sweet love-ditties
> As their white wings flap or fold."

Two mutilated angels in terra-cotta, apparently of the school of Verrocchio, keep watch and ward over the farmhouse in niches on either side of an archway. A pleasant-looking old *contadina*, who was washing on the *aja* (threshing-floor), told us with some pride that there was a chapel where mass was said once a year for the dead buried there. "It has always been here—at least, when I say always, for 1,382 years," said she, counting the centuries on her fingers as though they were *centimes*; "and that *is* always, is it not, signora?"

We went in to see the chapel which has been modernised, but on lifting a stained and faded curtain of blue calico which covered the wall behind the altar, we saw a fine ancient fresco, evidently by a master hand of the early fifteenth century. St. Antonio is seated in the middle with God the Father above, and on either side stand three life-size saints. St. Stephen next the window was particularly beautiful, with a sweet, solemn face one never tired of looking upon. The old woman knew nothing of its history, save that it was *roba antica* (old stuff), and that her *padrone* had put the curtain there because the saints were *schifoso* (dirty). He had intended repainting them, but artists were people without any conscience, or else their colours cost a lot of money; so the blue calico had been bought as a way out of the difficulty. Fortunately the pot of whitewash had not been thought of!

A little higher up the view is lovely. The valley we had just left forms a perfect V, with the grey tower and picturesque arches of St. Antonio rising in the very centre, like a watch-dog set to guard the pass; further down the long line of the monastery of Sta. Lucia crowned the brow of the hill to the left, and the background was formed by the broad plain of the Arno, bathed in a golden mist, while Monte Morello made a violet-grey mass in the far distance.

After climbing another hill the castle of Malmantile is seen standing out against the blue sky in solitary grandeur. The view thence is extensive and imposing; the barren, rolling hills seem endless as we look over the Val di Pesa, and far-off St. Miniato al Tedesco

> "lifts to heaven
> Her diadem of towers."

> "Risiede Malmantile sovra un poggetto:
> E chiunque verso lui volta le ciglia,
> Dice che i fondatori ebber concetto
> Di fabbricar' l'ottava maraviglia.

IN THE VALLEY OF THE ARNO

"L'ampio paese poi, che egli ha soggetto
Non si sa (vo' giuocare) a mille miglia:
Ve l'aria buona, azzurra oltramarina:
E non vi manca latte di gallina."

"Malmantile is placed on a hillock, and whoso turns his eyes that way will say that the founders were minded to make the eighth wonder of the world. The vast territory subject to the castle is not known (I bet) for a thousand miles round. There is excellent air and a blue sky, and even the milk of hens is not wanting."

Thus writes Lorenzo Lippi in *Il Malmantile Racquistato*, the mock-heroic poem, dear to every Tuscan, which has made the old castle celebrated. It needs a Tuscan to wade through 428 pages full of not only Tuscanisms, but Florentinisms, if I may coin the word. The painter, famous for his wit and power of repartee, used to stay in a villa near by with his friend Alessandro Valori, and employed his leisure hours in writing the poem on Malmantile, which word signifies a worn-out tablecloth. The proper names in the poem are nearly all anagrams, more or less witty, and the allegory seems to point the moral that those who lead a life of feasting and gaiety generally die on a dunghill. The proverb, *Andare a Malmantile* (Going to Malmantile), is used as a gibe against avaricious persons who do not give their friends enough to eat.

From the archives in Florence we learn that on the 5th of May, 1424, "The Most Honourable Ten, overseers of the city, of the districts of Pisa, Pistoja, Volterra, and other places, made a statement to the Signory of Florence that the castle of Malmantile di Selva was unfinished and a discredit to the noble Republic, as well as a danger; so on the 16th of September of the same year a contract was signed and sealed between the Honourable Ten and Piero di Curradino, and Ambruogio di Lionardo, master masons, before the Florentine notary, Antonio di Puccino di Ser Andrea. The *maestri* undertook to finish the castle with battlements and towers similar to those of Lastra a Signa, and also to make a deep ditch round the fortress." There is a tradition that Malmantile was unsuccessfully besieged by the Prince of Orange and his Spaniards, but I can find no confirmation of it.

The old castle is in ruins, with wretched hovels, which have sprung up like mushrooms, tacked on to the walls. The people are miserably poor, but smiling and pleasant, and on our admiring the singing of a pretty girl, whose blue cotton frock was better made than those of her companions, her mother said, with evident pride, but with an accent which tried to be disapproving, "*Si, è come il cuculo, tutto voce and penne*" (Yes, she is like the cuckoo, all voice and feathers).

The sun was declining, and the *civetta* (passerine owl) was beginning to utter its melancholy cry, so with a last look at the picturesque old ruin we turned our horses' heads towards the City of Flowers, and drove home.

> "The skies yet blushing with departed light,
> When falling dews with spangles deck the glade,
> And the low sun had lengthen'd every shade."

Popular Songs of Tuscany

"*La gentil toscana*," as her friends lovingly call her, is certainly the land of song. Everyone sings, from the highest to the lowest, and all can join in the chorus of the popular *stornelli*—born, one knows not where—which crop up every spring with the flowers, and every autumn with the ripening grapes. It is difficult to get the people to sing their *rispetti* or *stornelli* for you. They will not believe that anyone can care for their *roba antica*, or old stuff; and as to repeating the words—"*Questo va in canto, in discorso non si può dire*" (This does for *singing*, but one cannot *say* the words), will be their answer. The peasants, the bricklayers, carpenters, etc., generally sing at their work, and the *stornello* particularly is pressed into every variety of service. The lover serenades his mistress with burning words of love; the disappointed suitor, as he passes the house of his successful rival, or of the faithless fair one, insults or upbraids with a *stornello;* two women quarrel—they instantly begin to *stornellare* each other, ridiculing personal defects, or voiding family quarrels in the choicest Tuscan.

The *rispetto* is, almost without exception, a love-song in six, eight, or ten lines. The music is melancholy, often in the minor key, and some of the old airs are like a recitative, the end notes being drawn out as long as possible; some of them sound like Eastern airs.

How it is that no musician has ever taken the trouble to note down the music of the *real* popular songs, I cannot imagine. Gordigiani, Campani, Palloni, and many other *maestri* have composed music to the old words, or to modern imitations of them, but their *rispetti* and *stornelli* are very unlike the genuine thing. The old airs are difficult to catch, and still more difficult to note; but I have succeeded in making a considerable collection, some from the peasants in the country, some from friends, and others from hackney coachmen, masons, etc., in Florence. The inhabitants of the San Frediano and San Niccolò quarters of the town are reckoned the best singers, and a guitar is to be seen in nearly every house on the southern, or unfashionable side of the Arno. New songs are composed by the people every year, and on fine summer nights one often meets a crowd of one or two hundred people silently following three or four men with guitars, and perhaps a flute. You ask an explanation. "*E Oreste che canta*" (It is Oreste who is singing) is the answer. Some of them have beautiful voices and sing wonderfully well.

I know of a young mason with a tenor voice who was offered £400—a large sum in Florence—if he would learn to sing for the stage; but he preferred his liberty, and refused. As the singers pass slowly through the streets, you hear the noise of opening windows far ahead, and occasionally a loud *bene!* or *bravo!* comes from above, generally acknowledged by the little band stopping a few minutes to finish their song. One of the well-known singers in Florence at the present moment unites the incongruous occupations of a butcher and a flower vendor. In winter he kills oxen and lambs, and in summer he sells flowers. When he sleeps I know not, as he sings nearly all night long in the people's *cafés*, or in the streets with his companions.

G. Tigri, one of the most elegant among modern writers, has made an excellent collection of the words of *stornelli* and *rispetti*. The *rispetto* may be defined as a respectful (*rispettoso*) salutation from a lover to his mistress, or *vice versa*. The following is an example:

> "Vi vengo a salutare, rosa gentile,
> Vera delizia del giardin d'amore.
> Decco qua il vostro servo umile e vile,
> Chi v'a donato la sua vita e il cuore.
> A voi s'inclina reverente e umile,
> Come si deve a un fedel servitore;
> Però ti prego, rosa colorita,
> Sarai cagion ch'io perderò la vita?"

("I come to greet thee, gentle rose, that solely
The true delight of love's fair garden art:
Look down upon thy slave, so poor and lowly,
Who hath to thee given up his life and heart.
To thee he bows him down in reverence holy,
Fulfilling so a faithful servant's part;
But yet I pray thee, rose of brightest hues,
Wouldst thou be cause that I my life should lose?")

Here is a charming description of the seven beauties a woman ought to possess:

"Sette bellezze vuol' aver la donna:
Prima—che bella si possa chiamare;
Alta dev' esser senza la pianella,
E bianca e rossa senza su' lisciare;
Larga di spalla e stretta in cinturella;
La bella bocca, e il bel nobil parlare.
Se poi si tira su le bionde trecce,
Decco la donna di sette bellezze."

("The perfect woman should have beauties seven:
Before she have the right to be called fair—
Tall she should be, without her slippers even;
Of red and white in which paint claims no share.
To shoulders broad a thin waist should be given;
From sweet lips, sweet and noble speech must fare:
If, besides these, she should be golden-tressed,
Behold the maid with seven beauties blessed!")

Again, the lover hears the moon lamenting the loss of two of her stars. She complains to Cupid, and refuses to remain in the sky:

"La luna s'è venuta a lamentare,
Inde la faccia del divino Amore;
Dice che in cielo non ci vuol più stare;
Che tolto gliel' avete lo splendore.

E si lamenta, e si lamenta forte;
L' ha conto le sue stelle, non son tutte.
E gliene manca due, e voi l' avete;
Son que' du' occhi che in fronte tenete!"

("The moon has come to make her lamentation;
Before the face of Cupid she doth bend her:
No more i' the sky, she says, she'll hold her station,
Because that you have robbed her of her splendour.
And still her loud lament on this doth bear,
That when she counts her stars, all are not there.
There are two missing—and the theft is thine:
They are the two eyes in thy face that shine.")

Generally speaking, the last two lines of the *rispetto* are repetitions in altered words of the two former ones. It is difficult to render the tender grace, the perfect simplicity, and the purity of language and of style, in a translation. Peasants, shepherds, and charcoal-burners in the Pistojan mountains speak to this day the Italian, or rather the Tuscan, of the great poets. They read Tasso in the winter nights, sitting round the big open fireplace; the scholar of the house reads aloud; and the verse of the gentle poet may perhaps live longer under the fir trees of the Apennines than upon the lagunes of Venice. The children learn long passages by heart, and the recognised declaration of love by a young peasant is his singing the *ottave rime* of Tasso under the window of the girl he purposes to court with a view to marriage. The songs which come from the mountains are not more remarkable for the beauty of their language than for their delicacy and the respect for women which they breathe. Thus:

> "Se dormi, o se non dormi, viso adorno,
> Alza la bionda e delicata testa—
> Ascolta lo tuo amor che tu hai d' intorno,
> Dice che tu ti affacci alla finestra;
> Ma non ti dice che tu vada fuora,
> Perchè la notte è cosa disonesta:
> Fácciati alla finestra, e stanne in casa,
> Perch'io sto fuora, e fo l' inserenata.
> Fácciati alla finestra, e stanne dentro,
> Perch'io sto fuora, e faccio un gran lamento."

> ("Sleep'st thou, or wak'st thou, sweet face of my dearest?
> Lift that fair head in all its delicate beauty—
> List to the love that to thy heart sits nearest—
> He tells thee that to look out is thy duty:
> But tells thee not to come out in the gloaming,
> For night is not the time for maiden's roaming:
> But look out from the casement of thy chamber,
> Because I stand and sing, nor think to clamber.
> Look from thy casement—to this prayer consenting,
> Because I stand without, and make a great lamenting.")

In autumn there is a considerable emigration of the able-bodied men from the hills above Pistoja, and the country round Siena to the Maremma, to find work. They push on as far as Elba, Corsica, and Sardinia, where they are employed as miners, wood-cutters, charcoal-burners, and road-makers. But the love they bear to their Apennines never waxes dim, and they generally keep together in bands from the same village or district. In spring they return with their carefully hoarded earnings to their families. This yearly wandering has given rise to many of their songs. The following is the parting song of a young lover to his sweetheart:

"Quando che mi partii dal mi' paese,
Lasciai piangendo la mi 'nnamorata,
Et l' era tanto bella e si cortese,
Chi prese a domandar della tornata.
E gli risposi con poche parole:
La tornata sarà quando Dio vuole;
E gli risposi con parole umile:
La tornata sarà fra maggio e aprile!"

("When from my village I was boun' for starting,
I parted from my love with salt tears burning,
So fair and courteous in that hour of parting
Was she, she questioned me of my returning,
And I made brief reply to my heart's treasure,
That my return would be at God's good pleasure;
And I made her reply, in humble way,
I would return 'twixt April-tide and May.")

The girl whose lover is gone sings:

"Come faranno i mi' occhi beati
A star lontan da voi cinque o sei mesi?
Come faranno, che so' innamorati?
A noia gli verran queste paesi:
A noia gli verran questi contorni:
Sempre pregherò l' ciel che tu ritorni.
A noia gli verran cheste giornate:
Sempre pregherò l' ciel che ritorniate."

("What will these eyes do, late so blest in seeing,
With my love from me five or six months parted?
What will they do, to whom love was their being?
How will they loathe the hamlet whence he started,
The country round about how they'll be spurning!
My constant prayer shall be for thy returning.
How heavily the days will pass, alack!
The while I pray Heaven for thy coming back.")

Her lover replies:

"Tornerò, tornerò, non dubitare,
Caro mio bene, non aver paura,
Che a breve tempo mi vedrai tornare:
Che impressa porto ognor la tua figura.
Allor ti cesserò, bella, d' amare,
Quando morto sarò in sepoltura."

("I'll return, I'll return; fear not that, my own dearie,
With never a doubt let thy heart be distrest,
That after brief absence again I'll be near thee,
And till then thy face I bear stamped on my breast,
Nor e'er will I cease in my heart's core to wear thee,
Till dead in the cold of the tomb I'm at rest.")

A number of the letters written during these long absences are in rhyme, either composed by the young people themselves, or, if they cannot write, by the village poet, who has a large custom, and for a few pence writes the letter in prose or in verse, and even paints some fitting symbol on the first page—such as a heart transfixed by a dart, two hearts bound by a chain, two vases of flowers, or two wreaths. Some of these letters have been collected and printed by Tigri and by Tommaseo. Those which invoke the aid of the swallow are particularly pretty, begging the bird who comes from the sea to stay her flight, and to give the disconsolate lover a feather from her lovely wing, wherewith to write to his love a golden letter; promising to give back the amorous feather to the swallow, and begging her to carry the letter safely to his lady love. Another complains that he tried to write the name he loves, but the pen was so full of melancholy and the inkstand of sorrow, that he never could succeed, adding that if the waters of the sea were ink, the earth paper, and all the grass that grows on it pens, he would still need more sheets of paper to tell the immensity of his love.

Many of the phrases and comparisons in these letters are taken from the old *rispetti* and *stornelli*, which every peasant learns by heart as a child, together with the proverbs in which Tuscany is so rich. Some, again, have doubtless descended for generations, and the lover has only to change a name, and the colour of the hair and eyes, to make his letter suitable. Others are descriptions of the Maremma and of the work doing, or of Rome, the "city of eternal beauty."

The *rispetti* have a likeness to the ancient *strambotti* (derived from Strani Motti), which used to be sung in Sicily in Manfred's time, and I believe that in some parts of Tuscany the peasants still use the latter name for their songs. They were successfully imitated by Pulci, Poligiani, and Lorenzo the Magnificent, some of whose sonnets are even now popular.

In the villages the old custom of *andare a veglia* still exists. At nightfall the young men go in companies to houses where there are young girls, to sing and dance; some of their dances are accompanied by songs, such as *La Galletta* and *La Veneziana*. The dancers sing two lines, and the musician then plays the *ricordino*, or *intercalare*, a sort of quick *refrain*, generally in the minor key, while the young people dance round him in couples. The following are favourite words to these dance airs:

"La bella ballerina è entrata in ballo,
Mirala un po' come la balla bene!
Mirala al collo se le' ci ha il corallo;
La bella ballerina è entrata in ballo.
Mirala al petto se le' ci ha il bel fiore;
La bella ballerina è col suo amore.
Mirala in dito se le' ci ha il diamante;
La bella ballerina è col suo amante,
Mirala in petto se le' ci ha la rosa;
La bella ballerina è fatta sposa."

("The graceful dancer hath come to the dancing.
Look at her—only look—how well she dances!
Look at her neck, what coral on it glancing!
The graceful dancer hath come to the dancing.
Look at her breast, how sweet a flower is there!
The graceful dancer now is with her dear.
Look at her hand, which rings of diamond cover;
The graceful dancer now is with her lover.
Look, how her rosy breast the roses hide,
The graceful dancer hath become a bride.")

Other dances, as the *Trescone*, the *Villan di Spagna*, the *Manfrina*, the *Marina*, the *Contradanza*, the *Bergamasca*, the *Paesana*, the *Milordina*, the *Moresca*, etc., have each their peculiar air, but no words; except the *Vita d' oro*, when the man sings on ceasing to dance:

"O vita d' oro, vita d' argento!
Dammi la mano, chè son contento!"

("Oh, life of golden, life of silver store!
Give me thy hand, and I will ask no more.")

The ancient custom of going round and serenading the young girls on the last night of April still lingers in some Tuscan villages. The old Florentine writers describe the splendid festivals in town and country for the *Calen di Maggio* and the songs called *Maggi*. The peasants in out-of-the-way villages still plant a branch of some flowering shrub before the doors of their sweethearts, or carry a kind of Maypole, *Maio*, adorned with fresh flowers and lemons, and sing in chorus, while the lover presents a small nosegay to his mistress:

"Or è di maggio, e fiorito è il limone;
Noi salutiamo di casa il padrone.
Ora è di maggio, e gli è fiorito i rami;
Salutiam le ragazze co' suoi dami.
Ora è di maggio, che fiorito è i fiori;
Salutiam le ragazze co' suoi amore."

("May Day is come—the lemon is in flower:
Greet we the house-master, in happy hour.
Now it is May, and blooms on boughs are hoar:
We greet each maiden and her bachelor.
Now May is come—earth its flower-carpet covers:
Our greeting to the young girls and their lovers.")

Till within a few years ago the young people of both sexes used to join together in companies on the evening of the 1st of May, and serenade their friends, or the *padrone*, or any other benefactor they wished to honour. They improvised *stornelli* and *rispetti* to the accompaniment of a violin, a guitar or two, and a tambourine, and wore bunches of gay-coloured silk ribbons on their hats and on their shoulders. The following is a serenade to a young married couple, probably the *padrone* and his young bride:

"Alzando gli occhi al cielo veddi il sole
Accompagnato da una chiara stella,
Che sotto gli occhi miei facea splendore:
Non ho mai visto una coppia si bella.
Scusin, signori, s'io ho fatto errore
Colla mia rozza semplice favella.
Colà verdeggia una fiorita rosa,
Donna gentile, delicata sposa:
Pregherò sempre la divina Madre,
Che faccia vi figlio che somigli il padre!"

("I raised mine eyes to heaven, the sun was glowing,
With but one star beside his course so fair,
That as I looked its splendour still seemed growing.
Never a couple have I seen so rare.
But pardon, signors, if I, all unknowing,
Have erred in this my speech so poor and bare;
So blooms a rose, the flower of summer-tide,
As does this gentle dame, this dainty bride;
Still will I pray to our sweet Lady-Mother,
A son to send, as his sire such another.")

When anyone begins to sing *stornelli* (derived probably from the word *storno*, which means to send back or re-echo), he generally starts with an invitation or defiance, to induce his companions to reply to his song. In the old times the accepted term was *Ecce*, and the answer, *Cominci* (begin). It was thus Burchiello, the celebrated barber of the Via Calimara, where the rich cloth merchants of Florence had their shops, used to challenge his friends to sing. Such men as Filippo Brunelleschi, Luca della Robbia, Orcagna, and Lorenzo Ghiberti, who made the doors of the Baptistery—doors, said Michaelangelo, worthy of Paradise—were the friends of Burchiello. Gifted with a fine voice and feeling for music, with a biting tongue and ready wit, the barber's songs were the terror of his enemies and the delight of the people. To this day a certain class of songs are called *Burchielleschi.*

Near the church of Santa Croce, where Simone Memmi and Giotto loved to work, was the beautiful Fabbrini garden, famous for its orange trees—so famous, that a street near was called "Canto agli Aranci" (Corner of the Oranges); and here it was that the *improvisatori* most loved to congregate and challenge each other to improvise to the guitar on any theme given by the bystanders. A certain Cristoforo, a Florentine, surnamed "l'Altissimo" (the Supreme), was a renowned *improvisatore* about 1480. Another *improvisatore* of note was a secretary of the Republic, by name Bernardo Ascolti. Lorenzo dei Medici was celebrated both for his skill as a musician and as an *improvisatore*, and used to sing with a friend surnamed "Cardiere," who bore him a good second. In 1600, Doni says that singing in the open air, in gardens and cool places, was most popular in Florence; and there existed a society of *letterati* who had raised the art of improvising in verse to the guitar to such a height that Leo X. gave them the permission to grant the title of poet, and a laurel crown, to anyone they considered worthy of such honour.

As late as 1725, Bernardino Perfetti, a Sienese, was crowned as an *improvisatore* at Rome, in the Campidoglio; and in 1776, Maddalena Morelli, of Pistoja, surnamed "Corinna Olimpica," achieved the same distinction for her wonderful power of improvisation. She had the additional honour of suggesting a heroine to Madame de Staël. Many women have been famous for the grace of their language and beauty of voice; and even in these prosaic times there are a few left, whose improvising can rouse large audiences to enthusiasm.

But to return to the *stornello:* it consists either of three lines of equal length, or of a short invocation or exclamation, and two lines by way of conclusion. The following is in common use as a *stornello* to start with, though the singer often improvises a polite defiance suited to his company:

"Ed io delli stornellì ne so tanti !
Ce n'ho da caricar sei bastimenti—
Chi ne vuol profitar si faccia avanti !"

("Of catches I know so many, so many—
Enough, I swear, six ships to load !
Step forward, step forward—who'd have any !")

At the end of all the *stornelli*, and of a few of the *rispetti*, there is a kind of *refrain*, or chorus, called a *rifiorita* or *passa gallo* (cock's walk), sometimes with words, sometimes without. The following is a favourite air for the *stornello a fiore*, so called because it must begin with the invocation of a flower or blossom :

"Fior di limone!
Limone è agro e non si puol mangiare,
Ma son più agre le pene d'amore.

(*Rifiorita.*)

"Sei bellina, lo sento, lo so,
Port' i cappelli alla roccoco!

"Fior di granato!
Se li sospiri miei fossero fuoco,
Tutto il mondo sarebbe bruciato.

(*Rifiorita.*)

"Piglia la rosa e lasciar star la foglia,
Ho tanta voglia di far all' amor con te!"

("Lemon blossom!
The lemon it is bitter, too bitter for eating,
But bitterer his pain that loves thee, sweeting.

"Fair is my darling, I feel it and I know,
And wears her hair dressed *à la rococo.*

"Pomegranate blossom!
If a flame of fire were the sighs I sigh,
All the world would be burnt thereby.

"Gather the roses, and let the leaves be,
Dearly I love to make love to thee!")

The following air is more popular in the city than in the country, and is often used for improvising insulting words, for which the common people of Tuscany have no little facility:

But the pretty and anything but insulting words which we give are often sung to it:

> "E questa strada, la vo' mattonare;
> Di rose e fiori la vorre' coprire;
> D'acqua rosata la vorre' bagnare.
> Tu sei bellina, tu sarai mia sposa,
> Tu sei bellina, l' idolo mio sei tu!"

> ("Of the street where thou livest, I'd fain have the paving.
> With roses and sweet flowers I'd cover it o'er,
> With water of roses, too, everywhere laving!
> For 'tis thou art my beauty—my bride thou shalt be,
> My beauty—I'll make my soul's idol of thee!")

At the risk of wearying my readers, I give this *stornello alla Pisana*, or according to the fashion of Pisa, where the street singing is celebrated, and all the songs full of flourishes (*fioriture*), turns, and runs (*girigogoli*). Take for example the peasant's song:

"Quando nasceste voi nacque un bel fiore.
La luna si fermò nel caminare,
Le stelle si cangiaron di colore.

(*Rifiorita.*)
"O Biondina, come la va,
Senza la vela la barca non va!"

("When thou wert born a flower came to completeness;
The moon stopped in its course, thy beauty seeing;
The stars changed colour at sight of thy sweetness.

"My fair-haired beauty, how is't with thee? say:
Without the sail, the boat may not make way!")

But my space will not allow me to give more examples of the innumerable words and airs of the *stornelli*. I must not pass over without mention the patriotic songs, nearly all dating from 1848. Curiously enough, there are hardly any *rispetti* or *stornelli* containing patriotic sentiments. A few mention the Turks and barbarians, and complain how they carried away "La Bella Rosina" to slavery; or a girl on shore curses the Turkish chains which keep her love from returning to her arms. These point to the old days of the Saracen or Sallee Rover, the constant and daring ravager of the Mediterranean shores in the fifteenth and two following centuries.

But 1848 brought new life to the patriotic sentiment of Italy, and quite changed for the time the character of its national poetry and music. Garibaldi became the hero and inspirer of popular minstrelsy, and those who joined him the objects of popular ovation. One of the best known and most popular of these patriotic songs is that of the Tuscan volunteers as they marched to the field of battle when the cause of *Italia una* hung in the balance:

L'ADDIO DEL VOLONTARIO

"Addio, mia bella, addio !
L'armata se ne va.
Se non partissi anch' io,
Sarebbe una viltà.

"Grandi saranno l'ire,
Grande il morir sarà ;
Si mora ! E' un bel morire
Morir per libertà !

"Non è fraterna guerra
La guerra ch' io farò ;
Dall' Italiana terra
L' estrano caccerò."

("Adieu, adieu, my fair one !
The army takes the field ;
If I did not march with it,
A coward I were sealed.

"Oh ! great will be our fury,
And great our death will be.
If death comes, 'tis brave dying
To set our country free.

"It is no war 'twixt brothers,
The war to which I go,
But from the land of Italy
To drive the foreign foe.")

So rang the chorus day and night for weeks and months as the volunteers marched through the ancient streets and squares of the City of Flowers, armed and banded for the first time, in the inspiring cause of "Italy one and free." Time brought some deceptions, some disillusions, and many disagreements and dissensions.

This same song made its appearance again in 1859; but since Italy has been united the various patriotic songs are seldom heard, and I only succeeded in obtaining some of the less-known ones from the son of one of the volunteers of 1848, who had learnt words and tunes from his father. The following is one of them, of which he only knew one verse:—

INNO DEL 1848

"L'han giurato, li vidi a Pont' Ida,
Giù calati dal monte e dal piano.
L'han giurato, si strinse la mano,
Cittadini di cento città !
Cara Italia, bel suol adorato,
Raserena la tua fronte addolorata.
Como, Brescia, Milano è varcato,
E fra poco a Venezia si va."

("They have sworn at Pont' Ida, I saw them,
The sons of the mountain and plain—
They have sworn, their hands grasped as they pledged them,
Five-score cities, brothers again !

Dear Italy, face of new gladness
  To the sons of thy love thou may'st show;
We have freed Como, Brescia, and Milan,
  And soon to free Venice we'll go!")

At the Pergola, on the evening of the 11th of September, 1847, violent enthusiasm was roused by a very fine cantata, written by M. Mabellini, called *Italia*, or *Sorrow and Hope*. I have often seen veterans' eyes dimmed with tears at the sound of those heart-stirring words and soul-moving music. It is printed, so I do not give it here.

Besides the *rispetto*, the *stornello*, and the patriotic song, there is the *canzone*, or song of less sharply defined character, but always local, of which, as I have already said, three or four new ones make their appearance every year. Should one of these happen to take the fancy of the public, it runs through Italy like wildfire. Now and then a Neapolitan song comes *viâ* Rome to Florence, when it is nearly always slightly changed in rhythm, generally to its advantage; but usually the songs are composed in and about the City of Flowers. They seldom last more than six months, and are then completely forgotten—so completely, that after a few years a new tune is sure to be composed for any words that hit the public fancy. One of the Neapolitan songs just mentioned held undisputed sway in the streets of Florence and in the villages along the Arno for nearly a year: a case of almost unprecedented popularity. I have no doubt that many of my readers have heard the air; indeed, it has, I believe, since its sudden spring into popularity, been *arranged* (*i.e.* spoilt) by a Neapolitan composer:

PALUMELLA

"Palumella, zompa e vola,
Sulle braccie di Nenna mia.
Che taggio a dicere, che non mo moro.
Palumella, Palumella, pensaci tu.
Tra la la.
"Io ne vengo da Palermo
Pe trovar la Nenna mia,
Ma gli occhi lucidi son malandrini,
M'hanno rubato, m'hanno rubato, lu cor a me."

("Woodpigeon, woodpigeon, up with thee—off with thee,
Fly to the arms of my Nenna, my pet :
Tell her the word I send—how still I'm true to her,
Woodpigeon, woodpigeon, do not forget.

"Soon I'll be back again, back from Palermo,
To tend my own Nenna, the girl I love best ;
Though those bright eyes of hers, thief that she is for it,
Have stolen the heart of me clean from my breast !")

A few years ago a song came out in Florence which had immense vogue, partly from its own beauty, and partly on account of the half-romantic, half-comic story attached to it. It was reported that a well-known "cabby" of Florence, whose stand is at Santa Trinità, had fallen desperately in love with a Nubian or Abyssinian girl, one of a batch sent over by the Khedive for education in Florence, and that he had written the following song in her honour. His homage did not, however, touch her heart, as she soon afterwards married an officer in the army. The cabman is a first-rate player on the guitar, and has a nephew who sings remarkably well, with a very sweet, high, tenor voice. Be the story true or false, *The*

Queen of the Desert took the town by storm, and nothing else was heard from morning to night, and from night to morning. The beginning should be sung with fire and energy; the end slower and much emphasised:

REGINA DEL DESERTO

"Fuggiamo nel deserto,
Fuggiamo, amante mia,
Ogni sentiero è aperto,
Se tu verrai con me (*bis*).
Fuggiamo, perche vittima,
Io resterei con te !

"Come barchetto errante
Abbandonato al vento,
Noi non avremo avanti
Che un solo duce, il cor (*bis*).
Sia tempio il firmamento,
Sia nume, pace e amor.

"Il canto degli augelli
Sia l'inno tuo nunziale,
Un serto, su i capelli,
Di rose io ti farò (*bis*).
Regina del deserto
Io ti saluterò !"

("Forth to the desert lonely,
My loved one, let us flee :
One road for us, one only,
The road thou go'st with me (*bis*) :
Away ! a willing victim,
I'll give my life for thee.

"Even as a boat careering
  Before the wind is blown;
No pilot for our steering,
  But two fond hearts alone (*bis*);
Our church of Heaven's own rearing,
  Our god, Love, on his throne.

"The birds thy bride-song singing,
  Shall chaunt from leafage green;
With rosebuds of my stringing
  I'll crown thy tresses' sheen (*bis*):
My homage to thee bringing,
  I'll hail thee Desert Queen!")

The comic songs of Tuscany are *sui generis*. The airs are often very slight, and their charm entirely consists in the bright *espiègle* way of singing—or, I might almost say, reciting them. The bright eyes sparkle, and the mobile mouth is curved with laughter; even the guitar seems to be animated with fun and merriment. This summer *the* comic song is a bitter complaint that Mariannina had jilted the singer, ending in an imperative request to pull his leg hard when he gets into the railway carriage and goes to Turin—utter nonsense, but jovial, rattling music. Comic songs are generally restricted to one new one a year. I have chosen the following, which was popular some years ago, as a specimen, the air being prettier than the later ones:

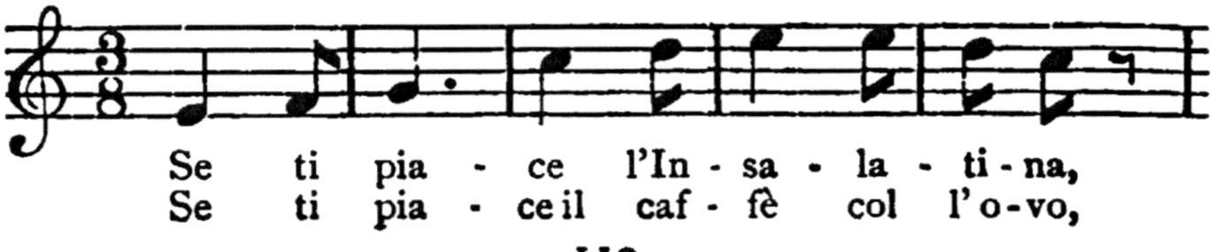

"Se ti piace l' insalatina,
Vieni in cucina; te la darò—
Ma no, non piangere nè sospirar.

"Se ti piace 'l caffé col l'ovo,
Ora ti provo se mi vuoi ben.
Ma no, non piangere, nè sospirar."

("If for salad you've a will, sir,
Come in the kitchen and eat your fill, sir:
Let's have no crying, no sighing, pray!

"If you've a fancy for coffee and eggs, sir,
I'll soon feed your passion, i' fegs, sir—
But let's have no crying, no sighing, pray.")

And so the verses run through the whole round of cupboard-love's temptations which a clever cook can hold out to a hungry wooer.

There are two other favourite comic songs—the first purely Tuscan, the second adapted from the Roman, and now popular in Tuscany—which admit of, and indeed require, infinite expression and archness in the singer.

"Mi son fatto un vestitino,
  Messo sì, pagato nò :
 E mi sento tirata di dietro,
 'He, ragazzina, pagate mi un po'.'
  'Vieni stasera,
   Domani sera,
  Sabato sera,
   Domenica, nò !'
 E così s'inganna l'amante,
  Prima di 'sì,' e poi di 'nò.'

"Mi son fatto un capellino,
  (Giubettino, giacchetino.)" (*etc., da capo.*)

("A duck of a dress I had ordered—
  Ordered it, yes—paid for it—no :
 When twitch, comes a pull at my jacket,
  And a 'Come, my girl, pay what you owe !'
   'Call in the evening—
   Call in the morning ;
   Saturday evening—
   Sunday—no go !'
 And so we go cheating our lovers,
  First with a 'yes,' and then with a 'no !' '

"A duck of a cape I had ordered,"
  Jacket, overcoat, etc.)

for the song may run through the whole contents of the female wardrobe.

Here is a Neapolitan comic song Tuscanised:

"Quand' un uom' ha mess' i baffi,
Ha bisogno di muliera :
Non c'è modo nè maniera,
Ma la femmina ci vuò.
Ma le femmine son tutt' amfanfari—
Sono tutt'uno culore ;
E quanno fanno amore,
Si lo fanno per se spassar—
Le femmine son fan—fan—fan—fan—
Sono tutt', etc. (*da capo.*)"

("When a youngster grows his whiskers,
'Tis women he must care for :
Without a why or wherefore
He must be a lady's man !
But the women they are humbugs ;
They're all bread of one baking :
And when love they are making,
They make it all for fun !
The women are hum—hum—hum—hum—
They're all bread of one baking.") (*etc., da capo.*)

But enough of attempts to translate the untranslatable. After all has been done that can be done by help of the most literal equivalent of the words, and most careful noting of the music, none but those who have lived among the Tuscan people can know what the Tuscan popular songs really are. Not till we hear them from Tuscan lips, to the simple accompaniment of the guitar, and perhaps a flute, in the open air, under the serene blue sky of evening, or the cloudless Tuscan moon, amidst the perfume of the lemon and growing grapes, and, above all, with the sweet spontaneous, unaffected Italian singing, like the singing of birds, so effortless it sounds and so irrepressible, can we really appreciate the charm of these songs—their simple pathos and old-world purity, their innocent playfulness, their shrewd humour, and their depths of sweet and sincere feeling.

VINTAGING IN TUSCANY

IN the lower Val d'Arno, overlooking the fruitful plain which extends from Florence to Empoli, stands an old villa, a long, low, roomy house, anciently belonging to the Arte della Lana, whose lamb bearing a banner over one shoulder is sculptured on various parts of its walls. In the twelfth century it was only a roof resting on high arches for drying the wool; then our host's ancestors bought it, filled up the arches, built a first floor, and gradually added wing after wing. The rooms are large and lofty, the staircase handsome, and the ceiling of one of the rooms is frescoed with Raphaelesque designs like the *loggia* in the Vatican. The house is full of old furniture, old china, and various Roman and Etruscan statues, and there is a splendid sarcophagus which was found on the property, for we are near Signa, the old Signa Romanorum of the legions. The villa, slightly raised above the plain, and about two miles from the Arno, is opposite Monte Morello, the weather-teller of the country round, as the old proverb says :—

"Se a Morello
V'è il cappello,
Non uscir
Senza l'ombrello." [1]

To the left, on the opposite side of the Arno, lies the town of Prato and the beautiful line of hills behind it, and further down the valley is Pistoja, and the Apennines in the distance. To the right we see Florence with its stately duomo and campanile, and in the background the hills of Vallombrosa. Behind the villa is a large garden, all the walks of which are shaded with *pergole* (vines on trellises), and from thence the ground slopes up to vineyards and olive groves, and to the wooded hills from the summit of which on a clear day one can discern the sea near Leghorn, some sixty miles off.

In this pleasant and picturesque old mansion were assembled a joyous company, mixed Italian and English, for the vintage of 1874. To the advent of the *forestieri* was ascribed by the courteous *contadini* the splendid yield of grapes, better than they had seen for twenty-six years.[2] On a fine September morning we started, Italian and English, men and

[1] "If on Morello
There is the cap,
Don't go out
Without your umbrella."

[2] That is to say, since the outbreak of the iodium. To give some idea of the virulence of the disease, the farms on this estate, though two less in number, used to produce at least two thousand *barile* of

VINTAGING IN TUSCANY

Face page 120

women, masters and mistresses, and servants laden with innumerable baskets, big and little, each armed with a rough pair of scissors, and our *padrona* leading the way, with her guitar, pouring out as she went an endless flow of *stornelli*, *rispetti*, and *canzoni*, in which Tuscany is as rich as in any of the country products, maize or figs, pumpkins or tomatoes, oil or wine, or grain, the Italians amongst us improvising words to the well-known airs. The vintage is always a happy time; everyone works with a will, and is contented and light-hearted. As Modesto, one of our men, said, "*Buon vino fa buon sangue*" (Good wine makes good blood).

The old *fattore* (bailiff), who had retired from all active work on the estate, except the management of his especial pets, the vineyards *alla francese* (vines cut low in the French fashion, and not allowed to straggle from tree to tree as is the Tuscan usage), was very great on this occasion. He pointed out trees he had planted, and works he had done, fifty years ago, before the *padrone* was born. The dear old man was now seventy-eight, and as brisk and alert as any of us; with an eye still bright, and his keen, humorous face as full of vivacity as the youngest. He was full of old proverbs and wise sayings, like all peasants of

wine; and in this, an exceptional year, the yield was only one thousand one hundred. One year, when the disease was at its height, they had five *barile* of stuff resembling mud! A *barile* holds fifty litres.

the Casentino, his native region, about twenty miles south-west of Florence; and looked sharply after all our workmen to see that each duly did the picking of his row of vines. He was struck with great admiration at the way in which Englishmen, and women too, worked, and quite concerned for the repeated drenchings in perspiration of a strenuous old gentleman of the party, remarking gravely, "*Questo povero Signor Antonio! ma suda troppo!*" (This poor Mr. Tom, he sweats too much). He chuckled when we got hot and red under the burning sun, gracefully putting it to the ladies, "*Il sole d'Italia vi ha baciato*" (The sun of Italy has kissed you). By eleven we were thoroughly tired, and went to rest under the scanty shade of the olives and fig trees with our guitar. One of the young peasants had lost his grandfather in Russia with Napoleon I., and we called him up, and told him to sing about the great general. He sung to a favourite *stornello* air:

"Guarda, Napoleon, quello che fai;
La meglio gioventù tutta la vuoi,
E le ragazze te le friggerai.

"Napoleon, fa le cose giuste,
Falla la coscrizion delle ragazze,
Piglia le belle, e lasciar star le brutte.

"Napoleon, te ne pentirai!
La meglio gioventù tutta la vuoi;
Della vecchiaia, che te ne farai.

"Napoleon, non ti stimar guerriero—
A Mosca lo troveresti l'osso duro,
All' isola dell' Elba prigioniero."

("While you go our youths collecting,
All our pretty girls neglecting,
Pause, Napoleon, and beware.

"Deal more justly with all classes,
Make conscription of the lasses—
Leave the plain and choose the fair.

"Napoleon, if with ruthless hand,
Of its flower you mow the land:
In old age you'll pay it dear.

"Boast not, tyrant, of your glory,
Moscow's plains were grim and gory,
Elba was a prison drear.")

Twelve o'clock brought a welcome arrival—lunch from the villa. Grape-picking is a capital sharpener of the appetite. We were soon reclining—*sub tegmine fagi*—round a steaming dish of *risotto con funghi*, and a knightly sirloin of roast beef, which would have done honour to old England. A big *fiasco* (a large bottle bound round with reeds or straw, and holding three ordinary bottles) of last year's red wine was soon emptied, well tempered, I should say, with water from the neighbouring well. At a little distance the labourers in the vineyard were enjoying the unwonted luxury of a big wooden bowl full of white beans crowned with *polpette*, little sausages of minced meat and rice.

We first gathered all the white grapes. These were transferred from our small baskets to big ones, placed at the end of each row of vines. These bigger baskets were then carried on men's backs to the villa, where the grapes were laid out to dry in one of the towers, on *stoje*, great trays made of canes. Here they are exposed to sun and air for some weeks, when they are used for making the *vin' santo*. After the white grapes were gathered, we fell to on the black, of the choice kinds, the "San Giovese," the "Aleatico," the "Colorino," and the "Occhio di Pernice." These also were destined to be exposed on *stoje* in the same manner. They are used as *governo*, that is to say, when the new wine is racked for the first time these choice black grapes are put in, so as to cause another fermentation; they at once deepen the colour of the wine and make it clear.

How melancholy the vines looked stripped of their grapes! The glorious white and golden, and pink and deep red bunches had given a beauty to the landscape which one did not realise until they were gone, and the poor vines stood bare. In our discussions about the progress of our work, the time of day often came in question. The old *fattore* was very anxious to know how we in England knew the hour, as he had heard that our churches did not ring the *Ave Maria* at midday or in the evening. He had, doubtless, a settled conviction that we were little better than heathens, but was too polite to say so. We explained that we had abundance of both big clocks and little watches; but he answered, "*Ma che*" (with a horizontal wave of the hand), "I have a watch too.

I set it by the *Ave Maria* and hardly ever use it. At midday, when the *Ave Maria* rings, we know we are to eat; and when we hear it at sundown, twenty-four o'clock, as we say here, we leave off work; and at one o'clock of night (an hour after sunset) it rings again so that we may remember our dead and say an *Ave* for them." All our arguments to prove that clocks and watches might be good substitutes for the *Ave Maria* were useless, and he remained stanch to his idea that England must be a wretched place without the *Ave Maria* — "*Si deve star male in Inghilterra senza l'Ave Maria.*"

At last the beautiful great white oxen, with their large, soft, black eyes, tassels of red and yellow worsted dangling about the roots of their horns and over their cool moist noses, came to the edge of the vineyard drawing a large vat (*tino*) fixed on the cart. Into this all the remaining grapes were thrown. A handsome lad of sixteen, after tucking up his trousers and washing his feet in a bucket of water drawn from the well close by, jumped atop of the vat and lustily stamped down the contents, singing as he plied his purple-stained feet:

"Bella bellina, chi vi ha fatto gli occhi?
Che ve gli ha fatti tanto innamorati?
Da letto levereste gli ammalati,
Di sotto terra levereste i morti.
Tanto valore e tanta valoranza!
Vostri begli occhi son la mia speranza."

("My lovely charmer, who hath made thine eyes,
That fill our bosoms with such ecstasies?
Their glance would draw the sick man from his bed,
Or haply pierce the tomb and raise the dead.
Oh! my sweet love, thy beauty and thy worth,
Are all my hope and all my joy on earth.")

Of such tender sentiment and musical sound are the songs of the Tuscan "roughs." These songs are most of them the composition, both words and airs, of the peasants and artisans who sing them. The hills round Pistoja and the streets of Florence ring with an ever-renewed outpour of such sweet and simple song.

The *padrone* prides himself much on his fine breed of oven, and told us the old Tuscan proverb, *Chi ha carro e buoi, fa bene i fatti suoi* (Whoso has cart and oxen does good business). When the last load of grapes was carted off we returned to the villa, where we found all hands busy in the great courtyard of the *fattoria*[1] on one side of the villa, emptying the grapes and must out of the vats with wooden *bigoncie*, high wooden pails without handles. These are carried on men's shoulders, and their contents poured into immense vats (*tini*) ranged all round the courtyard under covered arcades. In our wine-shed (*tinaia*) there are about fifty of these, containing from five to fifty butts each, besides three large square reservoirs of

[1] The *fattoria* comprehends the farm-buildings, cellars, granaries, bailiff's dwellings, etc., attached to a villa, just as in the Roman times the "Villa Rustica" was attached to the "Villa Urbana."

stone each holding three hundred barrels. The bubbling and boiling of the fermenting wine fills the air, and the smell is almost strong enough to get drunk upon. The men often do get tipsy, if they remain too long treading the grapes, or drawing off the new wine. But here it is an article of faith that the perfume of the must is the best medicine, and people bring weakly children to tread the grapes and remain in the *tinaia* to breathe the fume-laden air and eat of the fresh fruit; for at vintage-time no peasant or *padrone* refuses grapes to anyone who asks. They say that *il buon Dio* has given them plenty, and why should they in their turn not give to those who have nothing? I suppose this universal readiness to give is one reason why there is so little stealing here. You see vines full of fruit close to the roads, and quite unprotected by any sort of fence, and yet no one of the country-side ever takes them. There are, it is true, certain *malfamati* villages, whose inhabitants have the reputation of thieves, and against these, and pilferers from the large towns, the vineyards are guarded by men armed with guns, with which they keep popping the night through. At times you see twenty or thirty poor people standing quietly looking on, until called up to receive their dole of grapes, with which they go away happy, with their graceful "*Dio ve ne renda merito.*" At home they will mix water with the must they squeeze out of their basket or apronful of such ungrudged gifts, and make *mezzo vino*, or *acquarello* (water and wine fermented together), for the winter. The same thing is done on a large scale at many *fattorie*. This mixture of wine and water is distributed to the poor in winter, and is the common drink of the workmen about the villa. After the first good wine is drawn off from the vats, the *vinaccia* (skins, grape-stones, and stalks) is put into the press, and the second wine pressed out. This is good, but considerably rougher, from the larger amount of tannin, due to the skins and stalks, than that which is drawn off from the vats after fermentation without any agency of the press. After passing through the press, the clots of *vinaccia* are again put into the vats, and water is poured upon them. In eight or ten days a fresh fermentation takes place, and the *vinaccia* is once more pressed in the wine-press. This gives *mezzo vino*, or *acquarello* (half-wine), not at all bad, but of course of insufficient body to keep through the summer. For this there is no want of demand at the villa. Besides the rations of the work-people, there are the *poveri del buon Dio*. In Tuscany there are no almshouses or poorhouses, save in the chief towns. Most villas have one or two days in the week when alms are distributed to all who come and ask. Here the gathering of poor occurs every Monday and Thursday, at ten in the morning. A hunch of bread, a glass of half-wine, and five centimes are doled out to every applicant, and on Christmas Day anyone who brings a *fiasco* has it filled with *mezzo-vino*, and gets half a loaf of bread and a half a pound of uncooked meat. Such has been the custom, I am told, for many hundred years.

Our happy holiday vintaging lasted for five days, and then we went to help the vintaging of one of the *contadini* of the *padrone*, a family that had been on the estate for two hundred and eighty years. All their vines were trained Tuscan fashion on maples, and we had the help of ladders and steps to gather the grapes. Half the grapes, and indeed half of all the produce of the land—grain, pumpkins, flax, fruit, or wine—belongs to the *padrone*, who pays all the taxes and buys the cattle. The *contadino* pays no rent for his house, which the *padrone* keeps in repair. The peasant gives the labour, and the master finds the capital.

This is, in rough outline, the system of *mezzeria*, or half-and-half tenure, still universal in Tuscany. Like all human things, it has two sides, and may be condemned as the most backward, or defended as the most patriarchal and wholesome of systems, binding landlord and tenant in the bond of an obviously common interest, and encouraging the closest and most familiar relations between the two. When the landlord is intelligent, active, and judicious, he may become a centre of enlightenment and improvement to his tenantry; but all his attempts must be made with the most cautious discretion, or he will infallibly frighten, and perhaps alienate, his tenantry, who are thorough Conservatives, and love *stare super antiquas vias*. Thus the best commentary on the "Georgics" is still agriculture in action in Tuscany, a passing peep into one of whose most pleasing chapters has been attempted in this paper.

Oil-making in Tuscany

"*La prima oliva è oro, la seconda argento, la terza non val niente*" (The first olive is golden, the second silver, and the third is worthless). Thus said the old *contadino* Bencino, quoting a Tuscan proverb, on a splendid, late November morning, whilst carefully gathering the olives into a queer wicker-basket which hooked into his belt. Shaped like a half-moon, and about three-quarters of a foot deep, it fitted close to Bencino's waist, and did not impede his movements or shake the precious fruit and bruise them.

We had driven out from Florence to a *fattoria* or large farm, in the lower Val d'Arno, to see the process of oil-making; as our host said, "*real* oil, not the fabricated stuff you poor people in England are used to. You shall see the olives squeezed and taste the virgin oil." We made rather a face at this proposal; but the beauty of the country soon drove all disagreeable ideas out of our heads.

After a lunch at the villa, an ancient and original place, with enough old furniture and old china in it to gladden the hearts of a dozen *bric-à-brac* hunters, we walked two miles through the woods, up to the *podere* (farm) of Bencino, one of the *contadini*, on the top of a hill. The view was astounding. Florence lay to the right, at our feet, the dark cupolas looming out grandly against the snow-covered hills of Vallombrosa rising behind the bright city. In front was the fruitful valley of the Arno, with glimpses of the river here and there glistening like silver, and the slender, leafless branches of the willow glowing scarlet and orange as they tossed in the breeze. The old battlemented walls of Lastra-a-Signa looked stern and weather-beaten as though still frowning defiance to the enemies of Florence, whose fate she shared in 1529, when the Spaniards, under the Prince of Orange, committed such atrocities that the peasants still scare naughty children with their name. An old Tuscan proverb says, *E meglio stare al bosco e mangiar pignoli, che stare in Castello con gli Spagnuoli* (Better to live in the wood and eat stone-pine nuts than in a castle with the Spaniards). Monte Morello and Monte Ferrato rose behind, and the villas dotted here and there on the dark hillsides gleamed out white in the brilliant sunshine. The picturesque little town of Prato, twelve miles away, seemed quite close, and we could distinguish the beautiful marble cathedral, in which Filippo Lippi worked so well, inspired by the lovely face of Lucrezia Buti, the young nun who left her cloister at Prato to follow the smooth-tongued painter. In the farther distance we could see the white peaks of the mountains of Carrara, and to the left rose the majestic and snow-capped Apennines, all rugged and intersected with deep valleys.

The road was steep, and we wondered how the noble, big, white oxen managed to drag the awkward, heavy, two-wheeled *carro* (waggon) up such an incline. The ground was arranged in terraces, each with a line of olive trees on the outside and a line of vines on the inside. The centre was ploughed and sown with grain, while the banks of the terraces supplied fodder for the cattle. A Tuscan *contadino* throws away nothing, and cultivates his *podere* like a garden.

The black shining olives hung thick on the slender branches, which bent low under the weight. The crop was abundant, "*una vera grazia di Dio*" (a real bounty of God), as Bencino said. All the *contadini* of this *fattoria*, whose *podere* was situated on the slopes of the hills, where the ground is stony, and therefore suitable for the cultivation of olive trees, were busily engaged gathering the fruit; the men up in the trees and on ladders, the women and children picking up those which fell to the ground. The bruised berries are kept apart, to make the second quality of oil. The trees are most carefully and severely pruned, hollow in the middle, to form a cup-shaped tree. *Agli olivi, un pazzo sopra e un savio sotto* (A mad man at the top of the olive tree, and a wise one at the roots), says the proverb.

Enough fruit had been picked for the day's pressing, so we climbed up the bare bit of steep road which led to Bencino's house, accompanied by the old man and his four stalwart sons, two of whom had served in the army without ever having a bad mark, as their father told us with considerable pride. The house stood on the brow of a hill, and was built round two sides of a square courtyard paved with bricks; on the third side rose a high wall, with an arched gateway over which was an old escutcheon, carved in stone, of the fifteenth century, with a lily and "S. M." entwined. A covered staircase outside the house led into a large room, with huge beams and rafters browned with age and smoke. The fireplace was immense, with seats in the corners. Here we found Bencino's mother, a ruddy, brisk old dame of near ninety; we wanted to know her exact age, but she could not tell us, and replied with a proverb, "*Gli uomini hanno gli anni che sentono, e le donne quelli che mostrano*" (Men count the years they feel, and women those they show); adding that she had "*molti, ma di molti anni*" (many, many years), and that those sad years when Carlo and Pasquale, two of her grandsons, were both away at the war, had seemed to her a lifetime. "Ah, Illustrissimo," said she to the *padrone*, with tears in her bright old eyes, "let us pray that these kings and great folk don't make any more wars. It would kill me and the *sposina* there (Carlo's pretty young wife), if he had again to put on his *bersagliere* coat." The poor old woman clasped her wrinkled brown hands, and the pretty *sposina* echoed, "Let us pray to God." We had to admire the baby's fat legs, and drink a glass of Bencino's *vino vecchio*, which was excellent, and then went down into the courtyard, and descended two steps into the *frantojo*, or oil-pressing room.

In the centre was an immense stone basin, in which revolved a solid millstone about five feet in diameter, technically called, I believe, an edge-runner, turned by a splendid white ox, which, to our astonishment, was not blindfolded. Our host told us that it was difficult to get oxen to do this work; it takes time and patience to accustom them to it. The millstone was set up on edge and rolled round in the stone basin, secured to a big column of wood which reached to the ceiling. The whole machine was most old-fashioned and clumsy, and the *padrone* said, laughing, evidently as old as Noah's ark. Into the stone basin, as clean as a dairymaid's pan, five sacks of olives were emptied, which, in a short time, were reduced to a mass of dark greenish-brown, thick pulp. Stones and all were mashed with but little noise, save the occasional lowing of the ox when his tasselled and ornamented nosebag was empty. When Bencino judged that the olives were sufficiently crushed, the pulp was taken out from the mill, with clean new wooden shovels, and put into a circular shallow basket with a large hole through the middle, made of thick cord fabricated from rushes grown in the Pisan marshes, and looking very much like open cocoanut matting. As fast as these *gabbie*, or cages, were filled, two men carried them on a handbarrow to the press in the corner of the room, and piled one on the top of the other under the press. Then began the hard work. Two huge posts clamped with iron support a colossal beam, through which goes the screw, finishing below in a large square block of wood with two square holes right through it. Into one of these Carlo stuck a long beam, to which he hooked a rope, the other end of which was secured round a turning pillar of wood some six or eight feet distant, with a handle against which the men threw their whole weight. With many groans and squeaks the big block of wood revolved to the right until all the rope was twisted round the pillar; then it was unhooked, the beam was lifted out of its hole in the block and carried on Carlo's stalwart shoulder to be inserted into the next hole, and the rope again hooked round the end of the beam; this process continued until not a drop more oil could be extracted. The press was then screwed back, the *gabbie* carried on the handbarrow to the mill, where they were emptied, and their contents again ground; then they were filled, and put under the press for the second time, when more oil came dripping out, but of inferior quality. The refuse that remains, called *sansa*, is almost black, and quite dry and gritty. This is sold for threepence or fourpence a *bigoncia* full, about fifty-five pounds in weight, for making soap.

Olives contain two-thirds of water and one-third of oil, which naturally floats on the top of the water, and Carlo Bencino was busily engaged in skimming it delicately off with a big tin scoop. He poured it through a funnel into a clean wooden *barile* (a small barrel with narrow ends held together by large, flat, wooden hoops, holding about thirty-six quarts); and when this was full he shouldered it, carried it off to the *chiaritojo*, or oil-clearing room, and emptied it into a large *conca*, a terra-cotta vase well glazed inside. The room, like everything else, was scrupulously clean, and paved with red bricks sloping towards the middle, where there was an underground marble receptacle, in case of an accident, such as the breaking of a *conca*. The temperature is kept as equable as possible, and in cold winter weather a brazier is lighted at night. Nothing spoils the look, though not the flavour, of oil so much as getting frozen; it becomes thick, and seldom quite regains its golden limpidity, even when treated by people who thoroughly understand it.

Ten or twelve *barili* of oil can be pressed in a day, and as all the other *contadini* of the *fattoria* bring their olives up to the press at Bencino's, oil-making goes on for some time when the crop is abundant. It is hard work, and must be done with cleanliness and nicety. At first our host had difficulty in getting the *contadini* to see the importance of separating the bruised from the fresh-picked fruit, and of keeping the press and implements clean. They thought it was only a whim, which they obeyed, partly from a sense of duty, but chiefly because the *padrone* is extremely beloved by his tenantry.

The jollity and fun of the *battitura* (thrashing), or of the vintage was wanting; the days were short and the wind cold, and, as Pasquale said, "one's throat is out of tune in winter, and without a song work seems dull and heavy; however, we make up for it at night when we have *pan' unto* (oiled bread)." We asked what this was, and he explained that during the process of pressing the *contadini* who made the oil always invited their friends to eat *pan' unto* or toasted bread dipped in the new oil. The old folk talk about the crops and family affairs, and the young people sing, dance, and make love. Girls here never dance out of their own homes or the houses of friends, and on *feste* and saints' days the young men dance together out of doors, and the girls look on. Another odd custom is that a girl who is engaged to be married either does not go to the *feste*, or, if she goes, she puts on her everyday working dress, and does not wear her best earrings and bright-coloured little shawl tied coquettishly across her breast. She keeps aloof from the general company, and her *fidanzato*, or affianced husband, does not talk to her.

The evening passes away merrily, for many of the young men play the guitar or the accordion, and almost all sing enough to join in a chorus. Some of the old *contadini* are renowned for their talent as story-tellers, but their tales are all about real people. No northern Italian has ever heard of a fairy or a hob-goblin, and ghosts are scarce, and are held in small estimation.

Our host insisted on our tasting the new oil, and to our surprise it was delicious, like a decoction of very aromatic herbs, and entirely free from the rank, nasty taste we generally associate with oil. We now understood why Italian salads are so different from ours, and how a *fritto*, or dish of fried meat and vegetables, comes to be so excellent in Tuscany. Coming back to the villa by twilight through the silent woods, at the end of our walk we met a joyous company going up to pay Bencino a visit, and eat *pan' unto.* They had two guitars and an accordion, and, after cordial and even affectionate greetings between them and the *padrone*, passed on, singing in chorus as they breasted the hill. One of the girls was very pretty, which we shrewdly suspected explained Pasquale's blushes, and the *padrone* said she was a good girl, and so he would allow the marriage. We noticed that our host addressed even men who were thirty years his senior as *figliuoli miei* (my sons), while a woman was invariably *bambina mia* (my little girl), unless he knew her name.

VIRGIL AND AGRICULTURE IN TUSCANY

AGRICULTURE in Italy, at least in Tuscany, has changed so little since old Virgil sang, that his descriptions would pass muster with any peasant of the present day. The "hardy rustic" still goes into the woods and seeks for an elm or, by preference, an oak, to fashion into a plough-beam, for a *stanga* or *stiva*, "*stegola*" (handle), not less than eight feet long, and for the earth-boards, called *orecchi*, "*aures*" (ears), and also for the share-beams with double backs, called *dentale a due dorsi* (*duplici aptantur dentalia dorso*), which hold the *gombere* (*vomero*), or large iron coulter for breaking up the earth, and the *vangheggiola*, or smaller one for making furrows for sowing. On the slopes of the hills of Fiesole the whole plough is often called *bombero* instead of *aratro*. The yoke is rudely made of lime or beech, and the capacious chimney of the peasant's house still affords room for seasoning the wood.

The *aja*, or threshing-floor, as of old, is made solid with potter's clay, and beaten hard. Virgil recommends a huge roller, which is an unknown implement in Tuscany. The careful peasant even now picks and chooses beans, maize, and such large seeds one at a time by hand, and the ancient theory that a fine crop of bloom on the walnut trees indicates a good wheat-harvest still holds good, witness the well-known proverb:

> "Quando le noce vengono a mucchierelli
> La va bene pei ricchi e i poverelli."[1]

I cannot recognise Virgil's names for olives, *orchades*, *radii*, or *pausia*, in the Tuscan *morinelle*, *infrantoie*, *rosselline*, *correggiuole*, or *pendoline* and *leccine*. The two first named are also called *morcai*, because they contain more oil than the others, and make more *morchia*, or pulp in the crushing-machine. They are larger olives, but not so aromatic in taste as some of the smaller sorts. The improved way of making an olive plantation is still to hew an old stock in small pieces for planting, when a young olive tree springs from the sapless wood:

> "Quin et caudicibus sectis, mirabile dictu!
> Truditur e sicco radix oleagina ligno."

Pliny says that olive-wood worked and made into hinges for doors has been known to sprout; but on propounding this to a Tuscan countryman I met with extreme disbelief.

Some rash innovators have lately suggested sowing

[1] "When the walnuts come in handfuls,
All goes well for rich and poor."

olive-kernels and grafting the young trees; but Tuscans do not like changes, and are apt to quote:

> "Chi lascia la via vecchia per la nuova
> Sa quel che lascia, non sa quel che trova."[1]

If Virgil found it impossible to enumerate the different kinds of grapes and their names, how much more so is it the case to-day? But his praises of the Falernian wine are well deserved. White Falernian is excellent, and has an aroma and bouquet of its own, withal strong and generous. Tuscany is deservedly proud of her *chianti*, and *vin santo* from any respectable *fattoria* is not to be despised. But the worst of Italian wines is, that you are seldom sure of getting the same two years running.

The manner of making wine has not changed since the time of Virgil. White oxen bring the grapes in a vat placed on an unwieldy, heavy ox-cart, painted scarlet, from the fields to the *tinaja*, where they are poured into immense open *tini*, or vats. Night and morning the bare-legged peasants stamp upon them to prevent the upper stratum of grapes becoming acid by too long a contact with the air.

Virgil's excellent advice about thoroughly seasoning and breaking up the land before planting vines is carried out to the letter in Tuscany, where the ditcher

[1] "Whoso leaves the old road for the new,
Knows what he leaves, but not what he may find."

makes a trench three feet deep and three feet wide, which is left open to sun, wind and rain for six months or a year before it is again filled in, after having been drained in a rough-and-ready manner by pitching all available stones into the bottom of the trench. Two *magliuoli* cuttings, or, better still, two-year-old rooted plants, *barbatelli*, are then planted on each side of the young maple tree destined for their support. If a vineyard is to be made, the quincunx system, recommended by Virgil, is always followed, and you will still hear the head of the gang of workmen saying, "they must be like soldiers, properly in line." A little further on you will see a sturdy peasant following the plough, and others sowing and hoeing over the field; one at least will be singing a *stornello* at the top of his voice. Their legs are generally bare above the knee, and *nudas ara, sere nudus* is at once recalled to your mind. Down in the valley, by the brawling streamlet, whose course you can trace far away into the blue distance by the double line of tall poplars glinting in the sun, grow the tall, graceful, blue-green canes (*Arundo donax*). What would they do in Tuscany without the *canne?* Hedges are mended, young trees staked, and vines trained on *canne*. They need no care, and are as useful as they are ornamental.

The warning against planting olive trees in the vineyards, for fear of fire, is no longer regarded; on the contrary, olives are very generally planted in the new-fashioned *vigne alla francese*, or vineyards according to the French system, partly because they give very little shade, and partly with an eye to the future, in case the dreaded phylloxera were to devastate Italy, when the unhappy proprietors would at least have their olive trees to fall back upon. The tree sacred to Pallas will grow on the wild mountain-side, in the *biancana* or white marl, which is so poor that even the vine needs a very large quantity of manure in order to succeed well. Virgil's advice to study the colour of the soil is borne out in the Tuscan proverb:

> "Terra bianca, tosto stanca;
> Terra nera, buon gran mena."[1]

Vines are still planted and trained as in Virgil's day; and, alas! his warning against the "poison of the hard tooth" of sheep and goats still holds good. Would that all goats had long ago been sacrificed to Bacchus!

The fashion, in Tuscany at least, and I believe more or less all over Italy, is to keep a herd numbering from ten to three hundred sheep or goats at your neighbours' expense. Hedges are ruined, forests denuded of underwood and young trees; and often it is the syndic of the village, or some important person

[1] "White earth is soon exhausted;
Black earth bears good wheat."

in the commune, who thus sets the law (for there is a law against permitting goats and sheep to injure other people's property) at defiance. Being persons of authority, they are not likely to be attacked for breaking the laws they ought to administer.

The care of vines, as Virgil says, is never-ending, the ground must be dug twice in the year. When the labour of the vintage is finished, that of pruning begins. If the Tuscans laid to heart what the poet so truly observes:

> "Be the first to dig the ground, etc.;
> Be the latest to reap the produce,"

the wine would improve. As a rule the grapes in Tuscany are picked too soon, with a consequent loss of saccharine and alcohol in the wine. The old saying, though, *Fammi povera, ti farò ricco* (Make me poor, I will make thee rich), is being more followed, the vines are more scientifically pruned and with better instruments.

The propagation of the vine is done in various ways. The *magliuolo*, which I take to be Virgil's *truncus*, is the most used. The well-ripened wood of the long branches of the vine is cut into lengths of about three feet, and nearly two feet is pushed underground with a long iron instrument, which has a deep slit at one end, like two fingers. Then there is the *propaggine* (*propaginis arcus*), which consists in arching a long vine-branch, and burying about a foot of it underground. When the roots are formed, this is severed from the parent plant; but they say the vine is not so long-lived as when treated in the first-mentioned way.

Cattle are a great resource to the Tuscans, and they take a legitimate pride in the noble white oxen from the Val di Chiana, with small heads and horns, large, liquid brown eyes, and soft, fine skins. I have seen some at the fair at Prato, standing over nineteen hands high, their beautiful heads decked with various-coloured bits of cloth and small looking-glasses, and round their immense bodies a scarlet sash to show off their girth.

These cattle are all stall-fed, as pasture is unknown in Tuscany, and it is generally the work of the women and children to collect the fodder, which varies with the time of year from grass and clover to vine, elm, and oak leaves. The calves are most carefully attended to, and Virgil's advice not to fill the pails with milk, white as snow, but to leave it all for the beloved young, is perforce attended to, as the large white breed are such poor milkers that they have but just enough for their calves. When a milch cow is wanted she is bought from the herds driven twice a year down from the Swiss Alps. But Italians use so little milk and butter, that in any out-of-the-way village it is impossible to buy either.

As to the horses, so beautifully described by Virgil that one recognises at once a first-class breed, their descendants are indeed degenerate! The Italian horse, generally speaking, is a wretched animal. Small, ill-made, cow-hocked, overworked and underfed, broken-in and made to do hard work at two or three years old, he is the type of what a horse ought not to be. Ponies are, however, excellent, but overdriving generally ruins their paces. They probably owe something to Eastern blood, as their heads, legs, and good hoofs recall the Arab.

Sheep and goats, as I have before said, are a real pest in Tuscany, and the municipalities are beginning to awake to the damage they commit. The milk-cheese described by Virgil is extremely popular to the present day. The sheep are milked, and the milk is slightly warmed over a fire; some *presame*, a mixture of rennet and the beard of the wild artichoke, is put in, and in four hours the milk is set. To make this into cheese is easy enough: it is put on an inclined plane of basketwork and gently pressed with the hands for some time. It seems some shepherds have a reputation for making far better cheese than others, which is attributed to their having hotter hands; I have, though, noticed that a pretty daughter often has a great deal to do with the goodness of the cheese.

Bees are often kept by the monks, and few things

are more picturesque and serenely beautiful than an old monastery garden in the springtime. The double avenues of dark cypresses, and a tangled undergrowth of rosemary, lavender, and China roses, the grass all enamelled with daffodils, primroses, and wild orchises, and the bees busily humming hither and thither, form a picture not easily forgotten. The hives are almost invariably made of the hollowed trunks of willow trees, closed at the top and bottom with boards, and the cracks filled up with clay; very like what is described in the *Georgics*.

Many of my readers must have often compared Virgil with Italy of the present day. The love of home and country, and the strong family affections which strike us to-day are described by the old Mantuan poet, in the most exulting hymn ever written in honour of a country.

> "But neither the groves of Media, that land of wealth, nor fair Ganges, and Hermes, turbid with its slime of gold, can vie with the glories of Italy. . . . Teeming crops o'erspread it, and the juice of the Massic vine; olive trees possess it, and goodly herds; hence comes the warrior-horse, that proudly bounds into the field; hence the snowy flocks, Clitumnus, and the bull, the chiefest victim, which, often bathed in thy hallowed stream, lead to the shrines of the gods the triumphs of Rome. Here is ceaseless spring, and summer in months where summer is strange. . . . Think too of so many

glorious cities and laboured works, so many towns piled by the hand of man on steepy crags, and the streams that flow beneath those ancient walls! . . . Hail, realm of Saturn, mighty mother of fruits, mighty mother of men!"

A Stroll in Boccaccio's Country

To lovers of Boccaccio the small streamlet Affrico which rises in the Fiesole hills and flows along the eastern side of the Campo di Marte, near Florence, will recall the *Ninfale Fiesolano,* its poetical descriptions of the surrounding country, and the impetuous love of the handsome youth Affrico for the bashful nymph Mensola: a love which aroused the dire vengeance of the chaste goddess Diana.

The destruction of the forests which once clothed the hills round Florence has changed the whole face of the land. Writers of Boccaccio's time speak of shady woods, of rills, springs, and lakelets, whose memory is only preserved in the names of various villas, and of farmhouses which once were villas, belonging to the great Florentine families—La Fonte, La Fontanella, Font' all' Erta, Il Vivaio, and others. Which was the

> " . . . bella e chiara fonte
> Di fresche erbette e di fiore adornata,
> La quale ancor dimora appiè del monte
> Cecer, da quella parte ove 'l sol guata
> Quand' è nel mezzogiorno a fronte a fronte. . ."

where Diana threatened her nymphs with death if they

listened to a lover's pleading, none can say. But Monte Ceceri is still the quarry whence Florence draws grey freestone for her palaces, and the Affrico and the Mensola still meander murmuring down to the plain, where they unite before falling into the Arno.

The view from the little bridge across the Affrico is enchanting. To the left the hills are studded with peasants' houses and with villas, many of them interesting from association with men great in story or in art. Far away rises Vallombrosa—sombre in its clothing of pine-woods in summer, white with snow in winter—making a background for the pretty little village of Settignano and the hills of Pilli and the Incontro. Tradition says the latter was the meeting-place of the gentle enthusiast St. Francis, who so loved animals that he spoke of the birds as "our sisters," and of St. Dominick, the fanatic instigator of the horrible massacre of the unfortunate Albigense. In the plain lies the old villa Fontebuoni, where Benedetto Varchi wrote part of his *Storia Fiorentina*, and often entertained the beautiful courtesan Tullia d'Arragona, whose portrait at Brescia by Bonvicino justifies the passionate verses addressed to her by so many poets of that time.

Muzio wrote of those—

> " . . . occhi belli,
> Occhi leggiadri, occhi amorosi e cari,
> Piu che le stelle belli e piu che il sole."

Ercole Bentivoglio indited sonnets to her "celestial brow"; Bernardo Tasso discussed the theme of love with her in the presence of Niccolo Grazia and Francesco Maria Molza at Venice, and called her "la mia signora." Alessandro Arrighi praised her wise conversation and most rare beauty, and the

> ". . . bei costumi e 'l portamento adorno
> E col dolce cantare il dolce suono
> Che fan di marmo una persona viva."

Her mother, celebrated for her beauty, came from Ferrara; her father was Cardinal Luigi d'Arragona, son of the Marquis Gerace, natural son of Francis I. of Arragon, King of Naples, and of Diana Guardato. Tullia was born in Rome and educated in Siena and Florence, where she learnt music and developed a taste for literature. Filippo Strozzi was one of her many admirers, and in a long letter addressed to him, Francesco Vettori deplores that his name should be mentioned as one of the six champions who defied the world "according to the rules of ancient and glorious knights" in honour of "the Lady whose equal or like never has been, and never will be in any future centuries." Strozzi evidently listened to his friend's remonstrances, for his name does not appear among the signatories of the curious document.[1]

Tullia hired a villa on the banks of the Mensola in order to be near "Patron mio caro," as she called

[1] *Codex Rinnuccini.*

Varchi, who, in spite of the silvered hair he talks so much about, succumbed to the charms of the beautiful woman. Even after love had cooled into platonic friendship he continued patiently to polish and sometimes to rewrite, in his elegant scholarly language, the sonnets and verses of Tullia, who aspired to be a second Sappho.[1]

Her reputation as a poetess caused the Grand Duke Cosimo to excuse her from wearing the yellow veil, odious sign of her profession. She sent a sonnet with her petition, the original of which is in the State archives of Florence with

"Fasseli gratia per poetessa,"

in Cosimo's handwriting on the margin.

Poor Tullia died in March, 1556, in a small hostelry in the Trastevere at Rome, and was buried near the high altar of Sant' Agostino.[2]

Boccaccio may have seen the destruction of the stronghold of the Del Manzecca family, robber lords who harried the country round and levied toll on all who crossed the steep pass into the Mugello, for in 1348 the Republic of Florence lost all patience and ordered Castel di Poggio to be stormed and dismantled. Some hundred years later it was bought

[1] *Rime della Sigra. Tullia d'Arragona e diversi a Lei. Vinegia.* 1547.

[2] See "Un' Etèra Romana." Dr. G. Biagi. *Nuova Antologia*, August, 1886.

by the Alessandri, who repaired the castle and restored some grotesque frescoes in the chapel, now nearly effaced.

Below Castel di Poggio, Vincigliata towers high among pine-woods and cypresses—a remarkable restoration of an old feudal castle. If one of the Visdomini, the ancient lords of Careggi (Campum regis), as the place was once called, could return, he would feel himself quite at home in the fortress built by Mr. Temple Leader. The Usimbardi were the next owners of the castle and, of course, were at deadly feud with their neighbours of Castel di Poggio—thereby hangs a tale, a ghost story.

Giovanni Usimbardi, a friend of Dante, Cavalcanti, and other illustrious Florentines, had a daughter named Selvaggia, with whom the two sons of Del Manzecca fell in love. Simone, the eldest, asked her hand in marriage and was refused, so he stabbed her father, but fortunately only wounded him. The second son, Uberto, met the maiden at Mass in the church of Sta. Maria di Vincigliata, and by his beauty and gracious presence won her heart. Twice the life of Giovanni Usimbardi was saved in battle by an unknown knight, with a small knot of blue ribbon tied to the buckle of his breastplate. The second time the stranger was felled to the ground, and on his helmet being removed, Usimbardi recognised Uberto Del Manzecca, the son of his hated neighbour. The long-standing feud was made up and the wedding-day was fixed.

As Selvaggia stood at her casement, in bridal array, watching the lithe figure on the good black horse which knew the road so well down from Castel di Poggio to Vincigliata, she saw three men dash out of the wood. One seized the horse's bridle, the second pulled his rider out of the saddle, and before the young knight could draw his sword the third plunged a dagger into his heart. The murderer was Simone, Uberto's eldest brother.

The bridal bells tolled a death-knell, and Selvaggia sat with her lover's head in her lap until they took the body away for burial. She went raving mad, and died sitting at her window looking at Castle di Poggio.

And the peasants say that her ghost haunted the ruins of the old castle—her long fair hair floating behind her, and her white satin dress stained with blood.

There is every probability that Sir John Hawkwood, while in the service of Pisa with his famous White Company, sacked Vincigliata, as we read that the new owners, the Alessandri, rebuilt it in 1368. Some years later Niccolò degli Alessandri brought his bride Agnolleta, daughter of Bettino Ricasoli of Broglio, to the castle whence her granddaughter Ginevra rode down to Florence in great pomp to marry Giovanni de' Medici.

VILLA DI POGGIO GHERARDO

Face page 156

After the fall of the Republic the power of the Alessandri waned. In 1637 Messer Francesco, who cared for nothing but hunting, was living in a corner of the old castle with his young son and an old maiden aunt. A few years later the only inhabitants were the youth Giovan' Antonio and his page. In 1751 the entry in the church registry of Vincigliata runs: "No one lives in the ruined palace of the Signori Alessandri, but holy water is still sprinkled in the empty rooms when Easter comes round." [1]

Below Vincigliata, on an isolated hill jutting out into the valley of the Arno, between the streamlets Affrico and Mensola stands the square battlemented castle Poggio Gherardo, identified by students of Boccaccio with the "palagio" in which the joyous company of seven ladies and three youths took refuge when they fled from the plague of Florence in 1348.[2]

Tradition says that Palagio al Poggio, as the castle was anciently called, stood many a siege; and that when Sir John Hawkwood razed Vincigliata he destroyed the eastern *façade*, only partially rebuilt some two hundred years ago. It passed through several hands until in 1433 the Zati family sold it to Gherardo Gherardi. He changed the name from Palagio al Poggio to Poggio Gherardo, and his descendants held

[1] For a full account of Vincigliata see monographs by Baroni, Marcotti, and Leader Scott.

[2] See Baldelli, *Vita di G. Boccaccio*, Moreni, Repetti, etc.

the place for 456 years. It was bought by Mr. Ross in 1889.

Ruberto Gherardi wrote a long-winded but curious book in 1740, *La Villeggiatura di Majano*,[1] which has never been published, describing the hills of Fiesole, Majano, and Settignano, the villas, and the families they belong to. If not for nothing else, his MS. is valuable as suggesting, or rather asserting, that Giovanni Boccaccio was born near the banks of the Mensola. Till now Paris, and the Costa, near Sta. Felicita in Florence, have disputed the honour of giving birth to the great master of the Italian language. After a tedious account of various properties, Ruberto Gherardi mentions "a small villa near Corbignano, a townlet on the slope of the hill where rises the second branch of the torrent Mensola. . . . Descending but a few paces toward the plain we come to the villa and farm now owned by Sigr. Ottavio Ruggeri. This villa in ancient times was bought by Boccaccio di Chellino, perhaps when he first abandoned his native town Certaldo for Florence, and here was born in 1313 our master Giovanni, whose birthplace has hitherto been sought for in vain. . . . I am the more persuaded that our master Giovanni was born in this place from the fact that it lies about a mile from the valley of Ameto, under which name he speaks of himself in the *Commedia delle Ninfe Fiorentine*. He says

[1] MS. Gherardi, National Library, Florence.

that 'as a wandering lad Ameto often came to these woods to visit the fauns and the dryads who inhabited them; probably being descended from an ancient race of these hills, he was constrained thereto by an innate love and remembering his origin, he with pious memory came at times to do them honour.'"

With infinite patience old Gherardi identifies the different spots mentioned in *Ninfale Fiesolano*, *Ameto*, and the *Decamerone*, and Poggio Gherardo is generally accepted as the place Boccaccio had in his mind when describing the "place on a small hill, equidistant on all sides from any road," to which the joyous company of seven ladies and three youths walked on Wednesday at break of day to escape from the plague then raging in Florence. At two short miles from the city they arrived at the foot of the hill. "On the summit was a 'palagio,' in whose centre was a pleasant and large courtyard, with arcades and halls and rooms, each one beautiful and well ornamented with jocund paintings, surrounded by fields and with marvellous gardens, and possessing wells of freshest water and cellars full of precious wines, more suited to curious topers than to sober and virtuous women."

Here Pampinea was crowned queen with an "honourable and beautiful garland of bays," and here she commanded Panfilo to begin the series of immortal tales known all over the world as the *Decamerone*. At the end of the first day Pampinea ceded the garland, emblem of royalty, to "the discreet maiden Filomena," and the joyous company then went slowly down to a stream (the Mensola) of clear water, which, from a height near by, flowed among rocks and green herbage through a valley shaded by many trees. Here barefooted and with naked arms they descended into the water and disported themselves, until, the hour of supper being at hand, they returned to the palace and supped with great contentment.

The second day passed in like manner and Neifile was chosen queen. She commanded that there should be no story-telling on Friday or on Saturday, "days apt to be tedious to most folk because of the viands eaten thereon." It was done as the queen willed, and all looked forward with longing to Sunday. But she, thinking that having passed four days in the "palace on the hill" others might join them, roused the household at break of day, and sent on the seneschal to prepare the new abode she had already chosen. "Then with slow steps the queen, accompanied and followed by her ladies and the three youths, and led by the song of maybe twenty nightingales and other birds, walked towards the west by an unfrequented lane full of green herbs and of flowers just opening to the rising sun. Gossiping, joking, and laughing with her companions, she led them, after proceeding some two thousand paces, to a beautiful and splendid palace, before the half of the third hour had passed."[1]

[1] One and a half hours after sunrise.

The unfrequented lane may yet be followed, fragrant with wild violets and narcissi, leading through cornfields, bright with sweet-scented yellow tulips and scarlet anemones, from near Majano across the Affrico towards San Domenico. The hedges are tangled with eglantine and honeysuckle, and here and there an old oak recalls the forest that once existed. Every villa and every village within sight is connected with some illustrious name. Settignano recalls the great sculptor and architect Desiderio da Settignano, and Michelangelo Buonarrotti, who was put out to nurse at his father's farm near the village. He afterwards told Vasari, "I drew the chisel and mallet with which I carve statues in together with my nurse's milk." From Corbignano a family of sculptors emigrated to France, sons of Giusto Betti, known in French art-history as Les Justes of Tours. Those great artists Giuliano and Benedetto da Majano were born at Majano, and close at hand is the house which once was Macchiavelli's. Florentine platonism may be said to have had its stronghold among these hills. The three brothers Benivieni lived at villa Querce,[1] only separated by a small valley from Marsilio Ficino. One was an able doctor; another, a canon of San Lorenzo, called "my *complatonico*" by Ficino, had the courage to defend Savonarola. The third brother was a poet, whose *Canzone dell' amore celeste e divino*

[1] Now Montfort.

was thought worthy of a commentary by Pico della Mirandola. Devoted friends, they are united even in death, for they lie in the same grave in the church of San Marco in Florence. The family of Valori owned much property about here, and the villa Marmigliano still exists where the great platonist Marsilio Ficino was for so long the guest of Niccolò and Filippo Valori. Pico della Mirandola and Poliziano no doubt often came down from Fiesole to visit their friends, and in the ninth book of Ficino's letters (No. I.) he describes a walk on these hills with "our Pico" and their conversation about a salubrious villa. The latter fixed upon a building hard by as fulfilling all his desires, when Ficino tells him that "it is said to have been built by that wise man Leonardo Aretino, while just beyond was the abode of Giovanni Boccaccio." Below, to the left, is the Salviatino, once belonging to Duke Salviati, whose good old wine is recorded in Redi's jocund poem "Bacco in Toscana."

> "Where the hewn rocks of Fiesole impend
> O'er Doccia's dell, and fig and olive blend,
> There the twin streams of Affrico unite,
> One dimly seen, the other out of sight,
> But ever playing in his smoothen'd bed
> Of polisht stone, and willing to be led
> Where clustering vines protect him from the sun.
> Here, by the lake, Boccaccio's fair brigade
> Beguiled the hours, and tale for tale repaid."

Thus sang Walter Savage Landor, whose villa "Il

Frusino"[1] stands just above the small plain where once was the take of the Valley of the Ladies.

But we must return to the *Decamerone*. When the queen left the first "palagio" on Sunday morning at sunrise she led her companions "to a most beautiful and sumptuous palace raised somewhat above the plain on a small hill. Entering in and going all over it, and seeing the large halls, the cleanly and well-decorated rooms, fully stocked with everything pertaining unto rooms, they commended it highly and esteemed the owner to be rich and powerful. Then descending to see the vast and joyous courtyard of the palace, the cellars full of excellent wines, and the ice-cold water which welled up in large quantity, they praised it yet more."

The garden with wide walks covered by vine trellises and hedged in with white and red roses and jasmine, so that even when the sun was high there was scented and delightful shade, and the marvellous white marble fountain next called their attention. The overflow from the fountain, led in conduits about the garden, at last formed one stream and flowed down to the plain, where "with great force and no small gain to the owner it turned two mills."

The "sumptuous palace" with the beautiful gardens, which the seven ladies and three youths affirmed to be paradise on earth, has always been identified with

[1] Now belonging to Professor W. Fiske.

Villa Palmieri.[1] Here at the close of the sixth day the queen took off her crown of bays, and laughing, placed it on the head of Dioneo, saying, "It is time Dioneo that thou shouldst learn what an undertaking it is to rule and to guide women." And as though she wished to show how difficult that was, Eliza led off her six companions to a spot unknown to any—the Ladies' Valley. Here they found a small lake, and, having set their tire-women to watch that none should approach, took off their raiment and bathed. On returning to the palace they described the beauties of the valley, and the king ordered that next day the seneschal should prepare the midday repast by the lake, where the seventh day was passed in great pleasure, listening to the tales told by each member of the joyous company.

[1] Belonging to the Dowager Countess of Crawford and Balcarres. See Manni, Moreni, Baldelli, etc.

THE DOVE OF HOLY SATURDAY

SATURDAY in Holy Week is a great holiday for the Florentines, and still more for the *contadini*, or peasants, of all the country round. They come trooping into the city dressed in their holiday clothes, and the streets are crowded with the easy-going, good-natured, laughter-loving people, with jokes and proverbs on the tips of their tongues which they know full well how to apply. In old days spring and summer clothes were always bought on this day, and the shops were decked out and displayed their most tempting wares. This custom is a thing of the past, but the *colombina*, or dove, still speeds her fiery course down the centre of the old cathedral, and sets fire to the wonderful erection of squibs, crackers, and catherine wheels outside the great front door, piled up on an old triumphal chariot with four clumsy wheels, on the body of which traces of painting may yet be discerned. The dove flies at midday, but by ten o'clock the environs of the beautiful old marble Duomo are crowded, and from every quarter a never-ceasing stream of people pours in that direction. Many are the conjectures and the hopes that the dove may fly straight and well, as that indicates a good harvest, an abundant vintage, and a fine crop of olives. There is a tradition though that in the days of Napoleon I. the Archbishop of Florence and his clergy were threatened with heavy pains and penalties if the dove did not fly well, and that she sped like lightning down the cord in the church, and yet the crops failed. "*Ma chi sa,*" said my informant, "*se e vero? forse nò.*" (But who knows if this be true? perhaps not.)

By dint of patience and good humour we at last got into the Duomo, which bore quite a changed aspect. Every corner was crowded with people, save a narrow passage down the centre, from the front door to the high altar. To get a chair was a labour of extreme difficulty, and involved an amount of diplomacy impossible to any but a Florentine. The possessor of the chairs was captured, promised many things, and disappeared in an unaccountable manner round the huge pillars. He then reappeared, bearing a pile of chairs, but the crowd separated him from us, and his chairs were seized upon by other applicants. After nine or ten frantic efforts we got our chairs, much to the amusement of an old *contadino* and his wife, who, with various small grandchildren, had come to see the *colombina.* The old man had a wrinkled, expressive face, with very bright, acute eyes and iron grey hair, much such a face as Massacio loved to paint. He looked at us well, and then said in vernacular Tuscan, "*Chi ha pazienza ha i tordi grassi a un quattrin l'uno.*" (He who has patience gets the fat thrushes at a farthing apiece.)

We were so amused by this apt quotation of an old proverb that we made great friends, and took up his grandchildren on one of our chairs to see the show. The old woman was full of compliments and fears lest the children should be troublesome, but old Carnesecchi, as he told us his name was, had quite the old republican Florentine manners, respectful and civil, but perfectly self-possessed, and valuing his own personality. He invited us to come up to his *podere*, or farm, near Settignano, close to Michaelangelo's house, where, he said, laughing, the air is so *sottile*, so refined, that all the people are geniuses, only the world in general is not disposed to think so.

A stir in the crowd now showed that the Archbishop was coming out of the baptistery of San Giovanni, opposite the cathedral, and all heads turned towards the main door, where we soon saw the great white flag with the red cross appear, the flag of the people of Florence, followed by a long line of white-robed choristers singing. Other flags followed, then the canons of the cathedral in their picturesque long robes of dark purple, with white fur hoods, and lastly the Archbishop, a jewelled mitre sparkling on his head, a *pastorale* in one hand, all chiselled and set with precious stones, made by one of the famous old artificers of the fourteenth century, and bearing the sacred fire in the other.

Mass began at the high altar, but everyone's attention was concentrated on an unsightly high white post close to the marble balustrade which surrounds the altar. To this post was fixed a cord, which, suspended far above the heads of the people, disappeared out of the front door, and was fastened to the chariot outside the Duomo. A small white speck on the cord was pointed out to us as the famous dove. When the *Gloria* had been sung, a man went up a ladder with a lighted taper, and with great spitting and hissing the dove sped forward down the cord, a streak of fire and sparks. A stir and hum in the crowd, a few little screams from some of the women, and the dove vanished out of the door; and then there was a series of explosions from outside. In a few seconds the dove returned as fast as she had gone, and went back to the pillar of wood, where she remained fizzing for a time.

Then all the bells of Florence, which had been silent since twelve o'clock on Thursday, began to ring merry chimes, and the great organ pealed out a triumphant melody. We made our way out of the Duomo as fast as we could, and were in time for the last of the fireworks on the chariot; they made a tremendous noise, but as the sun shone brightly there was not much to see. The fireworks, piled up some twenty feet high, are arranged so that only half of them explode in front of the Duomo, the rest being reserved for the corner of Borgo degli Albizzi, where the house of the Pazzi is situated, in whose honour this custom was originally instituted. When all the squibs and crackers were finished, four magnificent white oxen, gaily decked with flowers and ribbons, were harnessed to the car, which moved slowly off with many creaks and groans round the south side of the cathedral towards the Via del Proconsolo. The crowd was immense, so we took some short cuts down the tortuous narrow streets in this old part of Florence, each of which has some passionate love-story or some dark tale of blood attached to it, and took up a favourable position opposite the entrance to the street of Borgo degli Albizzi, which is too narrow to admit the car. The four white oxen were unharnessed and taken away, and a cord being stretched from the door of the Pazzi palace to the car, another dove flew to the fireworks, and the popping and fizzing was renewed, to the intense delight of the crowd.

The dove had flown swiftly and well this year, so the *contadini* returned home joyfully, spreading the glad tidings as they went—"*La colombina è andata bene*" (The dove has flown well).

This ceremony is connected with the old and

noble family of Pazzi, whose ancestor, Pazzino de' Pazzi, so says tradition, was the first to scale the walls of Jerusalem and plant the Christian flag. Godfrey de Bouillon, to recompense such prowess, crowned him with a mural crown, gave him his own armorial bearings, five crosses and two dolphins, and bestowed on him three stones, supposed to have come from the Holy Sepulchre.

They were deposited in the church of S. Biagio, whence they were removed to S. Apostoli, and on the morning of Holy Saturday, the Archbishop, attended by all his clergy, goes to the church, and strikes fire from them. He then lights a taper, which is carried in procession to the Baptistery, and then to the Duomo, where the fire is blessed, and the devout light candles at it.

Gamurrini mentions that Pazzino de' Pazzi made a triumphant entry into Florence like a conqueror, in a magnificent chariot, and with a gallant company of youths around to do him honour; but old records contain no mention of a triumphal entry of any Pazzi, or of a mural crown, and R. Malespina and Monsignor Borghini both agree that the Count of Bari gave armorial bearings to the Pazzi in 1265. Travellers, too, say that the three stones are of quite a different nature from that of the Holy Sepulchre. They were probably collected on the Mount of Olives by some devout pilgrim of the Pazzi family, who brought them home as relics, and in process of time they have gained the reputation of being portions of the Holy Sepulchre.

Giovanni Villani, mentioning the claims of the Pazzi to be connected with this festivity, says: "The blessed fire of Holy Saturday is distributed throughout the city; an inmate from each house goes to light a taper at the cathedral, and from this solemnity arose great honour to the noble house of Pazzi through one of their ancestors, named Pazzo, who was tall and strong, and could carry a larger facine of tapers than anyone else; he was therefore the first to take the holy fire, and then he distributed it to others." When he died they say a car was made to carry them, and the real origin of the car being forgotten, it was transformed into a trophy, and the tapers into fireworks.

"Tantum ævi longinqua valet mutare vetustas!"

San Gimignano Delle Belle Torre

> "Thou hast a word of that one land of ours
> And of the fair town called of the fair towers;
> A word for me of my San Gimignan,
> A word of April's greenest-girdled hours."
>
> Swinburne.

For many miles round, San Gimignano is seen crowning the hill, its square towers breaking the sky-line in a quaint and picturesque manner. What vicissitudes have those high towers seen, and what famous men have passed through the old gate which still frowns defiance at the peaceful traveller!

Poggibonsi, the station for San Gimignano on the Florence and Siena line, has, like most Italian towns and villages, an interesting history. The old castle on the hill above the village, was taken and dismantled by the Florentines in 1257, to punish the people for their Ghibelline tendencies. Ten years later, Charles of Anjou spent four months in besieging it and, furious at being balked by so insignificant a place, ordered a strong fortress to be built inside the old castle walls, and left a governor there. As soon as Conradin arrived in Italy to try and wrest his birthright from French supremacy, the townspeople rose and driving out Angiovines and Florentines, they declared for Conradin. But when he succumbed at Tagliacozzo (August 23rd, 1268), and the Florentines defeated the Sienese on the heights of Colle, Count Guido di Monfort, governor of Tuscany for Charles of Anjou, joined the Florentine army, and Poggibonsi again underwent the horrors of a siege. The castle and the fortress were razed, and the inhabitants, deprived of all civil rights, were forced to quit their old city and descend into the plain near the torrent Staggia, where they founded the present townlet. The commanding position tempted the Emperor Henry VII., in 1313, to rebuild the old castle and surround it with stockades; he called it Poggio Imperiale, and lived there for two months.

On the road from Poggibonsi to San Gimignano, we passed near the mediæval castle of Strozzavolpe, once a stronghold of the Salimbeni of Siena. It is celebrated in the verses of Salvator Rosa, who painted some of his finest pictures there when staying with his friends, the Riccardi of Florence, who owned the place for several centuries. Further up the valley, we came in sight of the towers of unequal height, and the grey walls of the old town, standing out against the blue sky. The country is rich and smiling, and the *contadini* were busy tying up their vines and cutting green fodder for their cattle, while the hedgerows were enamelled with flowers glowing in the bright April sun. We soon came to the foot of the hill, and entering the more modern line of walls, built in the thirteenth century, drove up a narrow paved street and through a frowning double gateway, where the incline was so steep that our gallant little horses had to be encouraged with much cracking of whips and calling upon Sant' Antonio, into the Piazza della Cisterna; then, turning round the base of one of the square high towers, we found ourselves in the Piazza della Collegiata, in front of the old Municipal Palace, and transported back into the Middle Ages.

How out of place and unreal the people in modern dress looked! We pictured to ourselves the gallant train following Dante Alighieri when he came as ambassador from the city of Florence on the 8th of May, 1299. Dismounting in great pomp and state at the foot of the very steps we stood on, he went up into the Council-hall and by his fiery eloquence carried everything before him. Or the more martial escort of Niccolò Machiavelli, who came to San Gimignano in May, 1507, to raise a regiment of burghers to fight against Pisa in the Florentine interest.

Mounting the steep steps, we entered the great Hall of Council, decorated with several fine pictures from suppressed churches and monasteries, and with an immense fresco by Lippo Memmi, rather similar to his well-known work in the Palazzo Pubblico at Siena. At the feet of the majestic Virgin kneels the donor,

Messer Nello de' Tolomei, in his *podestà* robes; the canopy which shields her and the Infant Jesus is upheld by angels and San Gimignano. Under the Madonna, in Gothic letters, is written, "*Lippus Memi de Senis me pinxit*," and lower down, in Roman characters, "*Al tempo di Messer Nello di Messer Mino di Tolomei di Siena, onorevole potestà e chapitano del Chomune e del popolo della Terra di San Gimignano, MCCCXVII.*" This important work of art was damaged in 1461 by opening two doors into adjacent rooms, and Benozzo Gozzoli did not disdain to repair it, as is seen by the following inscription in the right-hand corner: "*Benotius Florentinus Pictor restauravit Anno Domini M°CCCC°LXVII°.*" A portion of the original intarsia-work benches are still in their places, where the councillors and rectors used to sit "decently habited with a hood and tunic or a chlamys of sober colour." The Municipal Council still meet here, and let us hope they lay to heart the apt sentence inscribed above the seat of the Provost of the Priors—

> "Priposto,
> Odi benigno ciascun che propone.
> Risponde grazioso e fa ragione."[1]

On one side of the great hall is the small and elegant tribune decorated with the line, *Animus in consulendo liber*, in intarsia work. Here it was that

[1] "Provost, listen benignantly to all who propound. Reply graciously, and do justice."

Dante advocated the cause of the Guelphs and induced the people of San Gimignano to send their representatives to a meeting of the Tuscan league at Florence. This is commemorated by an inscription on a marble slab, and close by is another in honour of the great modern Italian statesman, Cavour.

One of the doors which cut off the legs of the saints in the fresco by Memmi leads into a smaller back room, where the Provost and the Priors held their private meetings to discuss matters before laying them before the General Council. The intarsia benches all round the room are fine examples of 1475, and are decorated with verses written by Filippo Buonaccorsi, surnamed "Il Callimaco":

> "Pergite, Silviadæ, Romano sanguine creti,
> Pace frui, legesque sacras atque omnibus æquam
> Unanimes servare fidem : sed tollite, si quis
> Excitat adversos discordi fœdere cives,
> Et veterum moveant, et vos exempla novorum.
> Evellenda prius, sterilis quam crescat avena.
> Dogmata, ut hœc servant subsellia publica, cives
> Quîs cura est Silvi, sic pectore fixa tenete."[1]

[1] "Ye sons of Silvius, sprung from a Roman stock, continue to enjoy peace, and living in harmony to preserve the sacred laws and equal faith to all men. But if anyone endeavours to stir up your fellow-citizens by a hostile compact, away with him. Follow in this the example set by those of old and by those of modern times. The barren weed must be rooted out ere it spreads. And as these maxims are preserved (by being inscribed) upon these public seats, so do ye, O citizens, as you revere Silvius, keep them for ever in your hearts."

There are various frescoes in other rooms of the old palace; but the most interesting are downstairs in the chapel of the prison, now an office for the Attorney of the commune, who most appropriately sits under the effigy of the patron saint of all lawyers, St. Ives. This fresco is attributed to Sodoma, and is worthy of his hand. St. Ives is seated, hearing cases; and widows, orphans, and beggars are imploring him to see that justice should be done. Two angels uphold the arms of the Machiavelli family, from which we may infer that it was painted in 1507, when Messer Giovan Battista Machiavelli was *podestà*. On the opposite wall is an inferior fresco much damaged, with allegorical figures of Truth, Prudence, and Falsehood, the latter writhing under the foot of a seated and grave-looking judge. In one corner is written:

> "Per quel che pecha l'huō per quel patisce,
> Cava tu, verità, a la bugia
> La falsa lingua, qual sempre mentisce."[1]

The small courtyard into which this room opens is wonderfully picturesque. A *loggia*, upheld by slender columns, with traces of painting, runs round three sides on the first floor, and an old well stands on one side. The high tower, owing to a quarrel

[1] "For his sins, man suffers,
Tear thou out truth, from falsehood
The false tongue, which ever lies."

between the Council of the People and the priest of the adjacent Collegiate Church about ringing the bells, was only begun ten years after the palace, in 1298. So the Council determined to have their own bell-tower, and each *podestà* added to its height, affixing their arms to the piece built by them. It is 172½ feet high, and rests on a large arch; although it has been struck by lightning eleven times, it does not appear to have suffered.

The Collegiate Church stands at right angles to the Municipal Palace high above the piazza, a flight of twenty-five steps leads up to the doors, and, though much spoilt by successive alterations, traces of the original design by Matteo Brunisemd in 1239 are still apparent. The dim religious light of the fine interior is only sufficient to enable one to see that all the walls are frescoed. Benozzo Gozzoli, the great Florentine artist, painted the fresco of the martyrdom of St. Sebastian between the doors,—*Ad laudem gloriosissimi athletæ Sancti Sebastiani.* Paradise and hell are depicted on the side-walls by Taddeo Bartolo, of Siena (1393), and very quaint is the punishment of the gluttons, who sit round a sumptuously spread table, while hideous demons prevent them from stretching forth their hands to reach the food. The roof is azure blue, with gold stars, and frescoes by Domenico da Firenze (Ghirlandajo) Pier Francesco di Bartolomeo, also a Florentine, and

Sebastiano Mainardi, of San Gimignano. The nave on the left is frescoed by Bartolo di Fredi, of Siena (1356), but modern restoration has injured his work terribly. Opposite are scenes from the New Testament by Berna da Siena, who falling from the scaffolding, was killed in 1380, and Giovanni da Ascanio, his pupil, completed the work. "The people of San Gimignano were greatly attached to Berna," says Vasari, "and buried him with considerable pomp, not ceasing for many months to hang laudatory epitaphs in Latin and in the vulgar tongue round his tomb, the men of that town being much addicted to letters." Indeed, the quantity of inscriptions, epitaphs, and proverbs painted and sculptured in every conceivable place in the little town is astonishing.

The chief ornament of the church is the lovely chapel of Santa Fina, with Ghirlandajo's frescoes. Fina de' Ciardi, born of noble, but very poor parents, lost her father in early childhood, and by her great beauty and charm of manner attracted universal admiration. But she was extremely devout, and being ill, chose to lie on a narrow board without mattress or covering, so that at last her flesh adhered to the wood. On her mother's death, a charitable Donna Bonaventura took charge of her and her nurse, and soon afterwards St. Gregory appeared to the young girl in a dream and announced her approaching death. On the 12th of March, 1253, the bells, untouched by human hands, rang a solemn peal, and round the hard couch sprang up yellow wallflowers, *fiore di Santa Fina*, which to this day crown the towers of San Gimignano with a golden glory. Fina was dead; but, before burial, she raised her hand, and a blind deacon opened his eyes and saw, while her nurse Beldia regained her lost health. Other miracles followed, and in 1325 it was decided to erect a chapel in honour of the youthful saint, but owing to political events and to the plague nothing was done until 1465, when Giuliano da Majano was summoned from Florence to build it. Benedetto da Majano designed the beautiful altar of white marble; but unfortunately the sarcophagus, which contained the bones of Santa Fina, was removed in 1738 to make room for a new one, and now stands in the oratory of St. John. The two frescoes by Ghirlandajo are very lovely: to the right, St. Gregory announces to the sick girl her approaching death, in the clouds her soul is borne aloft by angels; while opposite is her funeral, and the hand of the dead saint is raised towards the blind deacon. On the tower in the background sits an angel tolling the bell, to commemorate the mysterious ringing of bells at the death of Fina. The roof of the chapel, which has been spoiled by restoration, was painted by Sebastiano Mainardi, pupil and brother-in-law of Ghirlandajo. In the sacristy is a wonderful, life-like bust, by Benedetto da Majano, of Pietro Onofrio, who in 1463 was elected by his fellow-citizens controller of the works of the church for life, an unheard-of honour, due to "his well-known and tried honesty and capacity; he died universally mourned in 1488, and his funeral was attended by a great concourse of people in St. Domenico, who saluted him as the Father of the Poor."

From the church door the view of the small square is striking. To the right, rises the majestic Palazzo del Podestà with its arched windows, iron balcony, and immense tower; on the left, the slender twin towers of the Ardinghelli, the great family whose quarrels with the Salvucci were an incessant source of trouble to their native city, still look down on the spot where, in August, 1352, the two handsome sons of Gualtiero degli Ardinghelli were beheaded by order of Messer Benedetto degli Strozzi, of Florence, Captain of the people, who espoused the cause of the Salvucci. Opposite is the first Municipal Palace, with its immense *loggia*, where justice was administered, and its high tower, called La Rognosa until 1407 when a clock was placed in it, and it became Dell' Oriolo. By an ancient edict, no tower belonging to any private person was allowed to exceed it in height (160 feet). After the erection of the other palace, this edifice was devoted to the reception of foreigners of distinction who visited San Gimignano. Now it has been turned into a theatre.

Turning to the left, we strolled down the picturesque streets and walking towards a long, low arch at the end of a lane, came to the small church of San Jacopo, commonly called "Il Tempio." Tradition says that a Messer Ruggiero Baccinelli went to the first Crusade, and returning thence laden with treasure, built, about 1096, a palace and church for the Knights Templar, who rendering themselves odious to the people, were turned out, their palace was pillaged and destroyed, and their lands and church given to the Knights of Malta. San Jacopo now belongs to the nunnery opposite, and the nuns pass unseen over the covered archway to hear Mass from the latticed windows in the ancient church, which is covered with faded frescoes of the thirteenth century.

Ivy and clematis hung in garlands from the arch, and as we passed under it a splendid panorama burst on our sight. To the left was the convent of Monte Uliveto, the townlet of Marcialla crowned the nearest hill, and Vico, a small yellow-grey-walled village, looked like an opal in the sun's rays. On the second range of hills lay Linari, and more to the right, surrounded with black cypresses, rose the tall campanile of San Leuchese; still further away was Pietra Fitta, and a villa and large park belonging to the Duke of

Aosta made a dark spot on the slope of the hill. The busy little town of Colle di Val d'Elsa lay more to the right, and beyond it range after range of pearl-grey and lilac hills melted away into the far distance. At our feet a shepherdess with her flock of goats and sheep passed slowly along, plying her distaff and singing in a sweet minor key about a knight, who met a shepherdess and warned her of a wolf. She laughed at his warning; but the wolf swallows her pet kid, and she begs the knight to pierce the brute's stomach with his glittering sword, promising to give him wool and goat's hair when she shears her flock. The knight says he is no merchant of wool or cloth, but that for one kiss of love from her sweet mouth he will do her bidding. He kills the wolf, the kid jumps out of its stomach into his mistress's arms, and all ends joyfully. Pear and cherry trees were in full bloom, glistening like new-fallen snow in the bright sun, while at our backs rose the irregular houses and tall towers of San Gimignano, and the old convent walls all aglow with Santa Fina's golden flowers, which scented the air and attracted butterflies and bees in swarms.

Not far from the Templars' church is St. Agostino, ugly enough outside, but containing many fine pictures, and, above all, the delightful frescoes by Benozzo Gozzoli, which cover the whole choir. In seventeen compartments he has represented the life of St. Augustine, from his first whipping by the schoolmaster of Tegaste to his death. We sat entranced by the *naïveté* and fun in the earlier scenes of the saint's career, as well as by the beauty of the compositions after his conversion. Every head must have been done from life and *con amore*. The same artist painted the fine fresco of St. Sebastian holding out his cloak to shield the pious San Gimignanese from the plague of 1464, over the altar, near which is a curious tombstone of the Benzi family; a skeleton, with the words *ibi, ubi*, and at the four corners of the tomb *nasci horror: vivere labor: mori dolor: resurgere decor*. Opposite is an altar dedicated to St. Bartolo, the favourite saint of this part of the world, son of Giovanni Buonpedoni, Count of Mucchio, and of Gentina, his wife. As a child, he was so amiable and charming that his companions named him "Angelo di pace" (angel of peace); in old age, he was called the Tuscan Job, from the patience with which he bore the horrible leprosy which afflicted him for twenty-two years. St. Bartolo died in 1299, aged seventy-two, and, by his desire, was buried in St. Agostino. So many miracles were worked at his tomb that a railing was placed round it in 1359 for safety, and in 1488 the commune of San Gimignano determined to set aside for three years the product of the grist tax, in order to erect a chapel worthy of his fame, and Benedetto da Majano was charged with the work. On the front of the marble sarcophagus is a bronze slab with the words, "*Ossa Divi Bartoli Geminianensis malorum geniorum fugatoris*," and on either side is sculptured an angel; below, in the "dossale" of the altar, are seated statuettes of Faith, Hope, and Charity, and a predella, with scenes from the life of St. Bartolo. Above the sarcophagus is a lovely roundel, an alto-relievo of the Madonna and Child, in a rich frame of cherubs' heads, flowers, and leaves. Two exquisitely sculptured angels stand in front, adoring the Virgin; on either side is a candelabrum of fine design; while from the arch above a curtain of white marble, delicately arabesqued in gold, hangs in folds so light that one might fancy it moved with the draught from the open door.

Many are the churches and convents in San Gimignano, and all contain fine pictures, frescoes, or sculpture; but we were bent on seeing the view from the Rocca di Montestaffoli, the castle built in 1354 by order of the Florentines after they had subjugated San Gimignano. High behind the Collegiate Church we climbed a rough road towards the ruin, and found ourselves on the threshing-floor of a peasant's house. We were welcomed by a smiling *contadina*, with several pretty children, one of whom was despatched to find Gigino to show us the way. A handsome young fellow came out of the stable and led us through the house, upstairs and downstairs, into the orchard, which covers about a quarter of a mile, and was once the courtyard of the castle. The machicolated walls are here and there interrupted by round towers, now used for storing hay, straw, beans, and agricultural implements. In the centre of the courtyard was a huge well, with a narrow neck and sides sloping outwards, covered with a trellis of peaches and vines. We mounted to the top of the largest tower, and were well rewarded for our climb. Towards the north was the Capucine Convent, surrounded with grey walls and dark cypresses, further back lay the town of Gambasso, and in the far distance the two tall towers of San Miniato al Tedesco stood out dark against the sky. Certaldo, the birthplace of

> "Him who form'd the Tuscan's siren tongue,"

was pointed out to us with pride by the peasant lad, and then a purple-black storm-cloud swept up, hiding the distant hills and towers and grey townlets, while in front the sun gilded the white villas. We turned southwards, and saw another storm rising. In a few moments the rival clouds hurtled and crashed together, and a thunderbolt fell straight as an arrow towards Colle. Gigino crossed himself and muttered a prayer, while we were lost in admiration at the play of light and shade on the rolling landscape, the weather-beaten towers of San Gimignano lit up with brilliant patches of yellow where St. Fina's flower was in full bloom, and the grey, crumbling walls of the old fortress garlanded with ivy and clematis, and fringed with irises, wallflowers, and peach-blossom. Where once was fighting and bloodshed, the peaceful olives shimmered silver-bright as their slender branches tossed hither and thither with the storm-wind, while the gladioli at their feet just showed pink flowers, and the star-like daisies made the earth lovely.

We found an excellent dinner at the primitive little inn next door to the Municipal Palace, and some Vernaccia wine, celebrated by Redi in his popular poem, "Bacco in Toscana."

"Se vi è alcuno, a cuì non piaccia
La Vernaccia
Vendemmiata in Pietrafitta,
Interdetto,
Maladetto,
Fugga via dal mio cospetto."[1]

We had remarked what a fine face the old hostess had, and she told us that she was the last descendant of Michaelangelo Buonarotti. Bitterly she complained that her great-uncle had left all his patrimony to the city of Florence to keep up the Michaelangelo Museum. "If he had left me only a few thousand francs I might have made *such* an inn. I have written to Umberto, the King, to beg him to lend me two thousand francs, to make my place

[1] "If there is anyone who does not like Vernaccia vintaged at Pietrafitta, interdicted, cursed, let him fly from me."

worthy of the strangers who come. You see, we were such simple folk in the old days, and now people are very luxurious. But he has not answered me," added she, with a sigh. We were, however, very comfortable, and the whole Giusti family did their best to entertain us, even getting us the municipal box at the theatre for four shillings. The principal actress had been with Salvini in London, and played Desdemona to his Othello. We retired to rest at midnight, but the rank and fashion of San Gimignano did not leave the theatre till past two.

Next day we drove to Volterra, one of our party quoting Swinburne's beautiful lines as we left the old town behind us:

> "And far to the fair south-westward lightens,
> Girdled and sandaled and plumed with flowers,
> At sunset over the sunlit lands,
> The hillside's crown where the wild hill brightens,
> Saint Fina's town of the beautiful towers,
> Hailing the sun with a hundred hands."

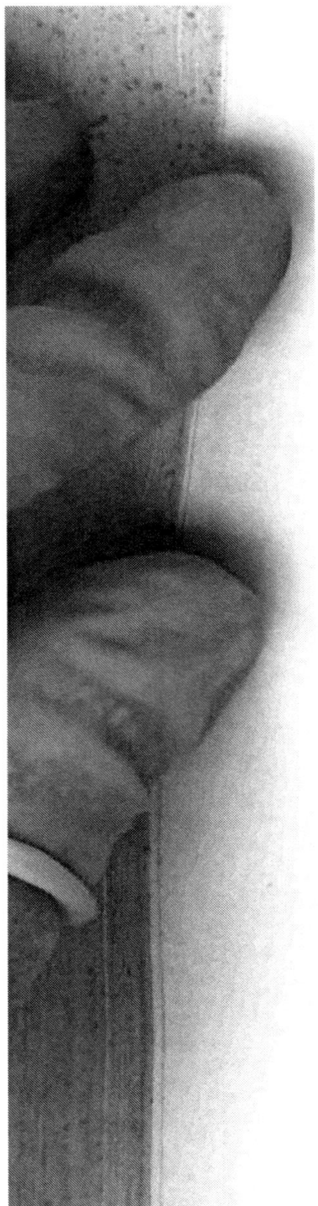

VOLTERRA

HE approach to the ancient Etruscan city of Volterra very fine; its towers and walls stand out sharply crescent shape against the sky, and the queer mass Monte Nero rises sheer out of the plain close ·. The whole country looks as though it had been ssed and tumbled about without rhyme or reason, d I wondered whether Martin had ever been here, his picture of "The Plains of Heaven" is curiously ke this savage, grand, lonely landscape. The hill emed endless as our horses toiled up the well-made ad and at length deposited us at the Albergo azionale, whose hostess was sadly disconcerted at r arrival, as all her best rooms had been ordered for e next day—rooms, as she informed us with pride, habited by the princes of Aosta not long since. he theatre, too, was open, and had attracted many ople from the country round.

Some mediæval writers gravely assert that Volterra wes its foundation to Noah, who, a hundred years ter the deluge, settled Shem in Asia and Ham in frica, and set sail for Europe with Japhet. He nded in Italy, and on the top of a high hill—

Volterra—he raised an altar to God. Others say that a grand-nephew of Noah, named Vul, was the real founder, whence comes the name *terra di Vul*, land of Vul. Some again resolve it into *Vola Tyrrhenorum*, or land of the Etruscans; but Dennis and other competent authorities regard Volaterræ as merely the latinised form of the Etruscan name Velathri, the syllable *Vel* or *Vul* being frequently found in Etruscan names, as Velsina, Vulci, Velimnas, etc. The rest of the word, *atri*, appears to have some analogy with *hat* or *hatkri*, found on the coins of Hatria, the Etruscan town which gave its name to the Adriatic, and to the *atrium*, or court, of Roman houses. Cramer and Millengen both infer from this analogy that Volterra was founded by the Tyrrhene-Pelasgi, when they left the shores of the Adriatic to settle in the land of the Umbri.

There is small doubt that Velathri was one of the twelve great Etruscan cities, but as little is known about her early history as about her inhabitants, those mysterious, highly civilised people called Tyrrheni by the Greeks and Etrusci by the Romans, whose language has been wiped out like writing off a slate, and is one of the enigmas still awaiting a solution. One can only gaze with wonder at the colossal walls,

> "Piled by the hands of giants
> For god-like kings of old,"

and at the cinerary urns which are dug up every day within the boundary of the ancient city, some of them sculptured with figures of rare grace and beauty.

The Piazza Maggiore, once called dell' Olmo, from a gigantic elm tree which grew where now stands the Palazzo Pubblico, built in 1256, is picturesque enough. Two *marzocchi*, or Florentine lions, guard the entrance of the palace, recalling the days when Volterra succumbed to the power and the wiles of the Republic, while armorial shields of the various Podestas, some in della Robbia ware, with the usual garland of fruit and flowers, decorate the front. If the stones of that old Piazza could speak, what tales of blood and daring, of treachery and self-sacrifice, they would tell! It was here that Bocchino Belforti was beheaded on the 10th of October, 1361. His father, Ottaviano, head of the Guelph party, a descendant of the richest and most powerful family of Volterra, rebelled in 1339 against the Ghibelline bishop and turned him and his adherents out of the city, burning and plundering their castles and possessions. He became absolute master of Volterra, and entered into a league with the Florentines, whom he supplied with money and men for their wars. In 1342 he sold his native town to the infamous Duke of Athens, contriving to retain the good graces both of the citizens and of the tyrant. The Florentines having proved themselves hard masters, Giusto Landini, a *popolano* (son of the people), raised the city against them in 1429. Clever, handsome, and courageous, Landini sent ambassadors to Siena and Lucca to ask for help, but with small success. Nothing daunted, he trained the people of Volterra, and prepared for a desperate resistance against Palla Strozzi and Rinaldo degli Albizzi, who were marching against the city, when the nobles, jealous of his popularity and power, asked him to come and confer with the priors and council in the Palazzo Pubblico. Little dreaming of treachery, Giusto went unattended, and no sooner had he put his foot over the threshold of the council-room than twenty daggers were drawn against him. Two of his cowardly assailants fell, but he was overpowered, mortally wounded, and thrown out of the centre window on to the pavement below. The death of the gallant young Landini was instantly communicated to the Florentine army, who marched into the city, imposed heavy fines on her citizens, forced them to build Il Cavaliere, a new fortress close to the old one, and deprived them of the privilege of electing their Podestà.

The Palazzo del Podestà, now the Prefecture and seat of the tribunal, was bought by the town of Volterra in 1223 for one hundred Volterrean *lire* from Giuseppe and Lottaringo de' Topi; and in the walls of the tower are still two ancient stones on which a mouse is rudely sculptured, so rudely that the lower is exactly like a huge pig. In old times the ons were here, and from the chapel, where the tched criminal passed his last hours, a trap-door his body fall into a subterranean room. It was ı this tower than Giovanni Inghirami let himself n by a rope, amid the jeers of the populace, in 2. Paolo Inghirami and Bernardo Riccoboldi, Volterra, with a Sienese and three Florentines, bought the right of excavating alum from the mune of Volterra, whose interests were said to e been entirely neglected by the secretary. Public ion ran high, and at length the matter was re-ed to the arbitration of Lorenzo de' Medici, who ded in favour of the lessees. Paolo Inghirami, named Pecorino, returned from Florence, and one day morning, coming out of the Duomo, "with a t superb air," says an old chronicler, "he being a and handsome man, with very bushy and arched rows, one Guasparri, having with him a dozen or e of those we call Lombards, tall men, as straight eir own pine trees and fairer than women, walked and down insolently on the Piazza. It being wn that this Guasparri was in league with the nies of the house of Inghirami, Paolo determined ake horse and retire to his country-place. But, ! his evil fortune decided that other councils ıld prevail, and he walked with most proud bear-into the Palazzo del Podestà, whence he sent to summon his adherents and servants. Now was the turn of Mancino degl' Incontri, his sworn enemy! On a sudden, a thousand voices cried, 'To arms!' In a few seconds the city was in a tumult; the great bell from the tower of the Communal palace tolled ominously and filled all souls with terror. Night put an end to this, but fires blazed in the streets, and you may well conceive that sleep fled the city. Next morning burghers and peasants, curiously armed, ran furiously up and down, crying with threatening voices for 'Il Pecorino.' He, who was no coward, hearing these loud voices, yet began to quail; and those who tried to preach peace were most evilly treated. The Podestà, not knowing what to do, at last signified that he would give up Paolo on condition that his life should be spared. Ferocious cries replied that no conditions would be given, and on a sudden the crowd forced the door of the palace and broke in. Romeo Barlettani, who of a truth was an excellent peace-loving man, put himself forward and tried to stop the people. He might have succeeded, but that a burgher, who owed him much money, knocked him on the head, when his body was thrown out of a window on to the crowd beneath. Paolo Inghirami, hearing the crash of the falling doors, rushed down some dark steps into a small room which served as a prison, but being soon discovered, defended himself with much desperation, running several of his ilants through the body. They hesitated, when ost villainous and ferocious idea seized them, and he twinkling of an eye sulphur and such-like stuff procured, and a large fire kindled at the door he prison. Paolo fell dead, and his fine body was led from the tower into the Piazza. Giovanni, younger brother, having taken refuge on the very mit, was made a butt for the arrows of the multi-; but being satiated by the blood already shed, people gave him his life, and let him down by pe from the high tower as though for a show and sement."

he old chronicle goes on to describe the anger orenzo de' Medici, and the determination of the entines to punish the people of Volterra. Duke lerick of Montefeltro and Urbino was their ral, and outside the gate of Selci, to the east of city, he gained a decided victory on the Poggio e Croci, so called from the many crosses erected the graves. To this day no plough has ever ed the earth, soddened with the best blood of terra. Internal dissensions, and the treachery of r Venetian and Milanese auxiliaries, betrayed the after a forty days' siege, into the hands of their ilants, who promised to refrain from plundering ill-treating the inhabitants. How ill this promise kept can be read in the history of those turbu-times; excesses only ceased, says an old writer, when a ribald soldier dared to rob God himself, seizing the holy vessel in the ciborium on the altar of the cathedral. At that moment a violent earthquake shook the whole city and did not cease until the terror-stricken thief had deposited his spoil on the altar, when he staggered out of the church like a drunken man, and threw himself headlong down the precipice near by. "Let all the enemies of God perish thus," piously ejaculates the narrator.

In order to secure their hold on Volterra, the Florentines ordered the destruction of the church of St. Peter and of the episcopal palace, which interfered with their erection of the fortress, still called La Rocca Nuova, a quadrangular building, in the centre of whose walls rises the tower, Il Mastio, which dominates Volterra, and was once celebrated as a State prison. The view from the top of Il Mastio is extraordinary: to the north the white villas of Nice can be seen on a clear day, and the curved shores of Genoa and Spezia; while the Maremma (where, according to the proverb, you get rich in a year and die in six months), stretches its rolling woods and green swamps for miles and miles towards the south.

Out of the bright sun one descends into those terrible dungeons; the lower ones only receive the air through a tube in the walls of enormous thickness, and in these cells, so small that you can hardly turn nd in them, many wretched victims passed years of uish. Giovanni and Galeotto de' Pazzi, two ng scions of the great Florentine family who ded the revolt against Lorenzo and Giuliano de' dici, were the first inmates. The last Gonfaloniere Florence, Rafaelle Girolami, spent many years in of them, and Vincenzo Martelli ended his life in Mastio for inditing a sonnet against Alessandro de' dici. Among other well-known names we find Pan-o Ricasoli, the famous Giovanni Bandini, and the brothers Lorenzini, sent here by order of Cosimo Third for corresponding with his wife, Margaret Orleans, after she separated from him and returned 'rance. In one of her letters to her husband she s, "not one hour passes that I do not hope to r you are hung. You, a flower of rue, God will have you, and the devil declines your company." enzo Lorenzini wrote his treatise on conic sections prison, without the aid of any books, and had it difficulty in persuading the constable of the er that those queer figures and lines were not gic.

unday morning broke grey and sullen; the mist driving in dense clouds from the plain beneath, ng the effect of a tossing, rolling sea, as we went High Mass in the cathedral, where the bishop was ciating it being a great Saint's day. Resplendent rimson satin, with a white mitre on his head, and surrounded by four canons in cloth of gold, the bishop sat on his throne with closed eyes, looking profoundly bored. At his feet, on the steps of the throne, were four choristers in red silk robes, and many other clergy stood round in white surplices. The Epistle and the Gospel were read by a canon, from the curious old pulpit in the body of the church, attended by a priest and a pretty fair-haired chorister-boy, who leant his curly pate on both hands as he put his elbows on the edge of the pulpit, and stared vacantly down on the congregation. Then the organ pealed forth, and the bishop slowly rose, leaning on a fine silver crozier, and for the first time raised his eyes. With a powerful yet musical voice he began a panegyric on those Italians who still worshipped the mortal remains of the Saints, pointing often to the high altar where stood a life-size silver bust. "O dearly beloved," he exclaimed, "you will hardly believe me when I assure you that there are atheists in this world who call us idolaters for adoring the sacred bones of Saints and Martyrs, but what do they worship? These heretical English come to Italy; they buy the greasy hat of Gasperone[1] for a fabulous sum, and take it back to their own country as a thing to be adored! The French, who, alas, have fallen away from their old love of our holy

[1] A famous bandit, whose peaked hat was, I believe, bought at Rome by an Englishman.

Church," here the bishop sighed deeply and paused, "creep on their knees to kiss the slipper of that arch-fiend Voltaire; and the Germans at Berlin, O my beloved—ah! you may well raise your eyebrows,—make pilgrimages to the cell of that unfrocked monk, Luther, whose very name is an abomination, and scrape the whitewash off the walls, preserving *that* carefully as a relic!"

The strains of Garibaldi's hymn and the shouts of *Eviva il deputato*, just outside the cathedral door, here drowned the voice of the irate prelate, whose face did not look pleasant as he wiped his brow with a red and yellow cotton handkerchief, which contrasted oddly with the splendour of his attire. I breathed more freely when we got out of the cathedral into the fitful sunlight among the joyous crowd—laughing and joking round the musicians, the long pheasant feathers in whose hats wagged gaily to the strains they were playing.

The people of Volterra are a fine race—the girls, in particular, are handsome, with singularly long almond-shaped eyes, straight mouths, and powerful chins, quite Napoleonic in cut. They are civil and pleasant in their manner to strangers, of whom comparatively few seem to come to Volterra, to judge by the absence of beggars. We paid fivepence each for a stall to hear *Poliuto* at the theatre Persius Flaccus. The orchestra was good, and the young prima donna sang charmingly and acted with feeling; but the chorus, though always in time and tune, were so funny in their dress and action, that it was impossible to look at the stage without laughing. Fashion in Italy requires that all hats should be cocked well over one ear, so the Roman Senators had put on their fillets *alla Bersagliera*, and the effect was more ludicrous than I can describe; those with curly hair looked like lop-sided cockatoos. The scenery, too, left something to be desired, as it represented mediæval Volterra, in whose narrow streets the Roman toga was rather out of place.

The museum in the Palazzo Desideri is admirably arranged, and reflects the greatest credit on the director. There are over four hundred cinerary urns or ash-chests, sometimes carved out of the local rock, *panchina*, but generally of alabaster; many still bear faint traces of gilding and painting. They are rarely more than two feet in length, and the reclining figure on the lid is always more or less grotesque, particularly the body, for some of the heads are evidently faithful portraits. The Etruscan manner of marking the age of the deceased is curious: on the urn of a youth is a four-leaved single flower; middle-age is symbolised by a double sunflower with wide-open uncurved leaves; old age by the same flower, with the leaves curved backwards and drooping. Many of the male figures make the Southern Italian sign against the evil eye, some hold a *patera* in one hand, which has a hollow in the centre underneath, into which the two middle fingers are inserted, leaving the first and fourth fingers sticking straight out, and thus making the *corne* or horns. Etruscan ladies were evidently learned, as many of the female figures have an open tablet or book in one hand; while the matrons have a *borchia*, a large round ornament held by a double chain, on the breast (in the collection of jewellery is a silver one found in a tomb), and hold in one hand a pomegranate, the emblem of fertility.

The subjects depicted on some of these urns are often very touching, as well as beautifully executed. Three, representing the Seven before Thebes, are remarkable as bearing on the old Etruscan gate of Volterra, the Porta all' Arco; on one is figured the ancient gateway with its three colossal heads (now unformed masses of stone, which were thought to be lions' heads, until the discovery of this urn). The centre head, the keystone as it were, is that of a female; the other two are heads of warriors. A favourite subject was the spirit of the dead on horseback, with Charun, a huge hammer over one shoulder in front, and a female figure, of some beauty, sadly following the jaded, dejected steed. This signifies that the evil deeds of the deceased outnumbered the good. When, on the contrary, the female figure precedes, the horse bears his head proudly, and steps briskly along, while

Charun follows, frowning and discontented, as the spirit has escaped him. The Etruscan Charun is by no means identical with the Charon of the Greeks, for the former was not only the ferryman (being sometimes represented with an oar, or a rudder), but also the messenger of Death, and the tormentor of the souls of the guilty. He is usually represented as a hideous old man, with flaming eyes and a ferocious expression, the ears of a brute, and often tusks like a boar. Sometimes he has wings with eyes in them, indicating superhuman power and intelligence. The hammer or mallet is his usual attribute, but occasionally he bears a sword, or a forked stick, perhaps equivalent to the *caduceus* of Mercury, or a torch, or snakes, the attributes of a Fury. But to me the most interesting urns were those depicting scenes of every-day life — touching, pathetic, and simple. The Etruscans certainly appeal to one's sympathies, and many of the figures are of extraordinary grace and beauty.

Outside the city, near the Porta San Francesco, is the convent of Sta. Chiara, now the Communal school. Below the convent garden are the most perfect fragments of the Etruscan walls, which had a circuit of six miles; one of these is forty feet in height, and one hundred and forty in length, the thickness of the wall being fourteen feet. Some of the blocks of stone are enormous, but rudely put together without a trace of cement; the masonry is irregular, one course often running into another, although a horizontal arrangement is always preserved. Following the road, we reached the church of San Justus and Clement, begun in 1628, and consecrated in 1775 to replace the old edifice, which dated from the seventh century, and had been totally destroyed by the encroachment of the ravines, which every now and then engulf land and houses on this side of the city. To the right are fragments of walls, and a half-buried arch stands in the middle of a cornfield, very solemn and very desolate; and a little further on are the *Balze*, where the ground sinks in fearful precipices, four hundred feet in depth and black as ink from the colour of the soil. A few poor cottages are standing within some twenty paces of the abyss, and a peasant who lived in one of them told me that he remembered, as a boy, walking straight across what now is a sheer ravine to the convent of the Badia for a daily ration of soup. When this gigantic landslip took place, he said Volterra shook to her foundations, "so terrible was the noise that we thought the last day had come, yet no one even thought of praying, we were too frightened."

Past the Fonte Grimaldringa, drinking, as in duty bound, of its celebrated water, and trying to trace the Etruscan gate which once stood near by, we went to the convent of La Badia, hastily abandoned by the monks after a landslip some twenty-five years ago. Picking our way through the excavations on the hill-side, one vast necropolis of Etruscan tombs, we climbed over a wall and got into the deserted cloisters. Most of the frescoes had fallen away from the walls; one alone remained in fairly good preservation—a monk's head, his finger to his lips, and the word *silenzio* written on a scroll, appropriate guardian for the sad, solemn place. Pushing open a rotten door, hanging by one hinge, we entered the church. Such a scene of desolation and destruction I never saw. The roof of the choir had given way, and in its fall had smashed the high altar, while great lumps of stucco had fallen off the square pillars of the nave, disclosing that once they were fine antique columns, probably from some temple. In the stained and cracked walls could be traced the original windows and arches, built in 1030, which had been filled up and altered in later times. All the friezes, bas-reliefs, and inscriptions, which adorned the exterior, have fortunately been removed to the museum in Volterra.

At the villa of the Inghirami are the *Buche dei Saraceni* (holes, or caverns, of the Saracens), the entrance to which is a little cave cut in the bank; but as one must creep on hands and knees down a passage tunnelled in the rock only three feet high, we took the vivid description of our guide on trust, and declined to wander, as he assured us we could in that uncomfortable posture, with a strong probability of losing our way in the labyrinth of passages which extend into the heart of the hill, no one knows how far. Tradition assigns these underground passages—occasionally, it seems, widening into large, low chambers—to the Saracens, those scourges of the Italian coast, who, beaten by Pope John the Tenth at Garigliano, about 920, were again signally defeated under the walls of Volterra. But it is more likely that the name derives from the family of Saracini, who in old times were lords of the castle of Miemo, an eagle's nest perched on the white peaks of the range of hills which runs from Monte Catini to Monte Vaso. These lordlings of Miemo often fought with the bishops of Volterra, and were not entirely subjugated until 1316. Now Miemo is only known as giving its name to a mineral called Miemite.

The Etruscan gateway Porta all' Arco, with its three featureless, mysterious heads, stands on the edge of the southern declivity of the town, and the view as one emerges from the dark passage, twenty-eight feet long, (for the gateway is double, united by massive walls), is very striking. The gate stands obliquely to the city walls, so that the approach to it is commanded on the right side, the one on which the assailants are unprotected by the shield, according to the rules of fortification enjoined by Vitruvius.

Not far above the gateway stands the baptistery of

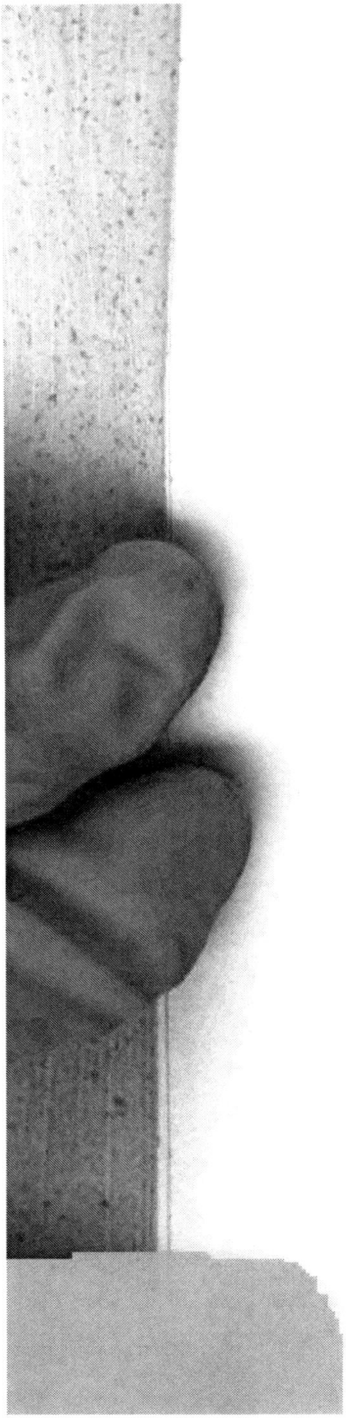

San Giovanni, an octangular building, of which Repetti says that, although no notice of it exists anterior to 989, he has no doubt it dates from a far earlier period. San Giovanni was probably lower once, and had no cupola, for in November, 1427, the magistrates of Volterra invited Pippo, Ser Brunelleschi, to come and consult about the covering of the baptistery, promising to satisfy all his demands. The old font is to the right of the high altar, and in a niche to the left is a priceless work of art which has been set up here recently, and thus saved from destruction—part of the high altar of the cathedral surmounted by a ciborium, which was removed in 1590 to an outhouse as "not matching the restorations." Unfortunately the crowning figure has disappeared, and the infant Christ is of modern work. The delicate chisel of Mino da Fiesole never carved anything more beautiful or more devout than the adoring angels at the four doors of the tabernacle, at whose foot are Faith, Hope, and Charity.

Facing the baptistery is the cathedral, where the clergy swore fealty to Charlemagne when he visited the city in the month of February 800. Tradition says that it was founded by Pope Siricius and the Emperor Theodosius in 390, but being a small square structure and inadequate for the congregation, Niccolò Pisano was chosen by acclamation as the architect in 1254, and enlarged it into its present form of a Latin cross. He also built the principal door, and the rose-window above. In 1580 the Bishop Serguido, with the help of Ferdinando dei Medici, made the splendid wooden ceiling, gorgeous with gilding and enormous busts of saints; the Virgin over the high altar is a fine piece of carving. It was then that the old altars were removed, but fortunately the curious old pulpit on four columns, resting on quaint monsters, and the beautiful marble candlesticks by Mino da Fiesole on either side of the high altar, were not also swept away.

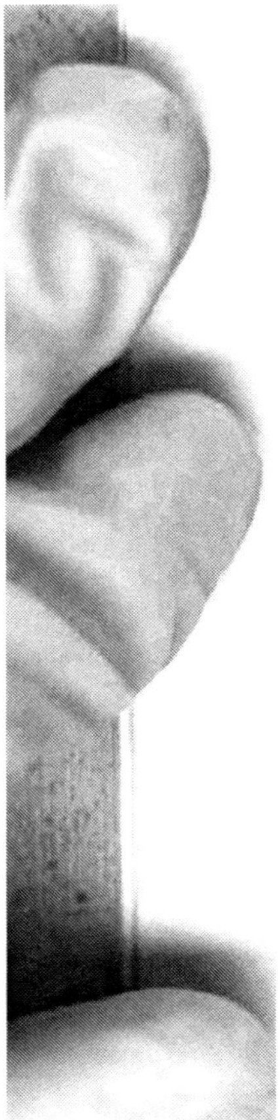

Mezzeria, or Land Tenure in Tuscany

The system of *mezzeria*, or half-and-half land-tenure, which prevails throughout Tuscany "was instituted," writes the late Marquess Gino Capponi, one of its most strenuous advocates, "in the palmy days of the Roman Republic when the plebeians obtained civil rights, but fell into disuse when slavery became general." In the fourteenth century, when the strong hill-castles of the robber lordlings were razed and their power was broken, it was again almost universally adopted, and a memory of its Roman origin still exists in the peasant's habit of speaking of themselves as the *gente* (the Roman *gens*) of their *padrone*, or landlord.

M. de Sismondi praises *mezzeria* in eloquent terms, while the Marquess Cosimo Ridolfi utterly condemns it, and advocates a return to *la grande culture*. He was answered by Signor Lambruschini, who pointed out that a day labourer has no interest in the land he cultivates, or in the success or the failure of the crops. "If you abolish *mezzeria*," he writes, "all those families, who, though poor, have a roof they can call their own, a field they can call theirs, and a master they love and bless; who, toiling and watching under rain and sun, hope, and pray to God, for abundant crops for themselves and for their master, will for the first time feel the pangs of envy and hatred, the shame and despair of being forced to beg, and to wait for work. At the same time we shall learn to dread meetings and strikes, such as occur in France and in England, the destruction of agricultural machinery, the burning of ricks, barefaced robbery and—as the last and miserable remedy—the poor-tax."

Theoretically, *mezzeria* is the equal division between landowner and peasant of everything the soil produces. The former brings the capital, the latter gives the labour. Every *podere*, or farm, the size of which varies considerably in different parts of Tuscany (from eight to thirty, or even forty acres), has on it a house, stables, and outbuildings, for which the peasant pays no rent. The necessary oxen, cows, horses or donkeys, are paid for by the landlord, and all gain or loss on them is divided between him and the peasant. The late Sir Henry Maine describes (*Nineteenth Century*, December, 1877) a state of doings among the South Slavonians and the Rajpoots, curiously like the life of the Tuscan *contadino* of the present day. The house community of the South Slavonians, despotically ruled by the paterfamilias, and the house-mother who governs the women of the family, though always subordinate to the house-chief, is almost a counterpart to the primitive custom still existing in Tuscany. In dealing with strangers the *capoccio*, or head-man, represents the family, his word or signature binds them all collectively, he administers the family affairs, he decides what work is to be done during the day and who is to do it, and none can leave the paternal roof, or marry, without his consent, ratified by that of the *padrone*. On Saturday night the various members of the family state their wants to him, and he decides whether they are reasonable, and whether the family finances permit of their realisation. The rule of the *capoccio* is a despotic one; I know the case of an old man, the head-man's uncle, who was kept for a time without his small weekly pittance for buying snuff, as a punishment for disobeying an order.

Every month the *capoccio* brings his book to be written up by the landlord or his factor, and half of whatever money he has encashed for milk, vegetables, fruit, and other minor products. Grain, pulse, wine, and oil are divided in kind, the landlord providing the necessary machinery for pressing oil and wine, and the vats for the fermentation of the grapes. If silk-worms are reared, the cocoons are sold by the landlord, who either pays the peasant his half share, or passes it to his credit in the books, which are audited once a year by a certified accountant, who reads over the items of debit and credit to each *contadino* in the presence of the *padrone*, and then appends his signature. Many of the peasants can neither write nor read, but their memory is unfailing and the slightest mistake is instantly detected.

The eldest son generally succeeds to the dignity of *capoccio*, although he may be passed over, and an uncle or a younger brother be chosen by the *padrone* to fill the position. The *massaia*, or house-mother, is usually the mother or the wife of the head-man, but occasionally of more distant kin. She rules over the women and keeps the purse for the smaller expenses of the house, such as clothes for the women, salt, pepper, and white rolls for the small children. All these are bought with the proceeds of the women's work, and the girls, from the age of fourteen, are allowed a certain time every day to work for their dowry.

The Tuscan peasant is a thoroughgoing conservative. He has not yet grasped the fact that railways and steamboats have brought about a change in the world, and hankers after a large extent of land on which to grow enough wheat for the year's consumption, being inclined to regard other crops as accessories. This does not suit the landowner, particularly as it is customary in Tuscany to grow wheat two, or even three, years running on the same land, with little or no manure, and the yield is, of course, miserable. It never occurs to the *contadino* to calculate the cost of tilling the ground, of sowing, reaping, and threshing; he will tell you that the labour of his family costs nothing. In vain you argue that the sale of other crops will buy wheat cheaper than he can produce it. "My forefathers grew their own corn," will be the unfailing answer; "what was good enough for them, is good enough for me." Bread is the staple food of the Tuscan peasant, and he is particular as to its quality, which is generally excellent.

A *podere* (I speak only of Tuscany) is divided into three portions, one of which is dug deep by the spade every year, when vines and olives are well manured. The less land a family have, particularly in the vicinity of large towns, the better it is cultivated; every square yard is turned to account, and the peasant becomes rather a gardener than a husbandman.

Notice to quit on the 3rd March is given by the *padrone* to the *contadino* (and *vice versa*) in July, when the division of the wheat is made; but should there be reason to believe that the latter will deal unfairly by the land, the *padrone* can delay giving notice until the 30th November. This is, however, seldom done, unless the peasant has behaved badly and forfeited all right to be treated with consideration. From the moment he has received, or given, notice to quit, he can neither prune nor plant, but he sows wheat and forage. His successor grafts and prunes the vines, and clears the ditches, and has the right to a room in the house after the 30th November. He only takes full possession on the 3rd March, when the animals (called *stime vive*), farm implements, hay and straw, stakes for vines and young trees, growing crops of forage, and manure (the *stime morte*), are consigned to him. All these are valued by two sworn valuers—one for the incomer, one for the outgoer. A peasant must hand over to his successor the same *stime* he received when he entered the farm; if there is a diminution, he must make it good; if an increase, the incomer pays him. The wheat, having been sown by the outgoing man, belongs to him, and he returns to reap and thresh it in July; but only the grain is his (his half share, of course), the straw belongs to the *padrone* and to the new peasant for the use of the animals. All this is very complicated and inconvenient, as often a *contadino* comes from, or goes to, a farm many miles away; much time is lost in going to and fro, and the land always suffers when there is a change of tenant. "Ogni muta, una caduta" (Every change is a disaster), says the proverb.

A *contadino* almost invariably chooses a wife from his own class, and from a neighbouring family, thus obeying the old sayings, "Donne e buoi de' paese tuoi" (Women and oxen from thine own country); and "Chi di lontano si va a maritare, sara ingannato o vuol ingannare" (Whoso seeks a wife from a distance will be deceived, or wishes to deceive).

After a due course of courtship—during which the

young man visits his *innamorata* every Saturday evening and on holidays, bringing her a flower, generally a carnation, or a rose, and improvising *terze* or *ottave* rhymes in her honour, which he sings as he nears the house—the *capoccio* dons his best clothes, and goes in state to ask the hand of the girl for his son, brother, nephew, or cousin, as it may be. When, after much talking and gesticulation, the affair is settled, a *stimatore* or *savio*, an appraiser or wise man, is called in, who draws up an account of the bride's possessions. These generally consist of a bed, some linen, her personal clothes, and a *vezzo*, or necklace of several strings of irregular pearls, costing from five to a hundred pounds, according to her father's wealth, or the amount she has been able to earn. The *vezzo* represents half the dowry, and those who are too poor to buy pearls have to be content with a necklace of dark red coral beads. The appraiser's estimate is consigned to the *cappocio* of the bridegroom's house, who keeps it carefully, as if the young man dies without leaving children, his widow has a right to the value of all she brought into her husband's house. If there are children, the *capoccio* is the sole guardian; he administers their property for them, unless the mother has reason to think him harsh or unfaithful, when she calls for a family council, who name two or more administrators. The widow may elect to remain in her adopted family, and look after her children, or she can return to her own people if they are able and willing to receive her, which is not often the case, as in Tuscany the *contadini* marry their children by rotation, so that the younger sons or daughters have to wait until the elder are settled in life. Widows with children do not often marry again, and folk-songs and proverbs are condemnatory of the practice :—

"Quando la capra ha passato il poggiolo non si ricorda piu del figliuolo" (When the shegoat has crossed the hillock, she forgets her young).

"Dio ti guardi da donna due volte maritata" (God preserve thee from a woman twice married).

"Quando si maritan vedove, il benedetto va tutto il giorno per casa" (When widows marry, the dear departed is all day long about the house).

When a marriage has been settled the bride's family invites the *capoccio* and the bridegroom to dinner to meet her relations. This is called the *impalmamento*, and many toasts are drunk to the health of the young couple, but the bride does not visit her future home until she is married.

The peasantry now generally observe the new law of civil marriage, but they still regard it as a mere form, and look on the religious ceremony as the important thing. The civil marriage is often celebrated three or four days before the religious service, and the girl goes quietly home to her father's house until the day fixed for the latter, which in some parts of the Val d'Arno takes place after sundown. The bride wears a black dress, with a white bonnet or cap and white gloves, and even in winter a fan is an indispensable adjunct to her costume. Bridesmaids are unknown, as no unmarried girl is ever present at a marriage. The bridegroom's mother, or the *massaia* of his house, stays at home to welcome her new daughter, whom she meets on the threshold of the house with *il bacio di benvenuto* (the kiss of welcome). At the dinner or supper, as the case may be, everybody in turn makes a *brindisi* to the young couple; but the female relations of the bride do not go to this dinner, and she makes up a basket of eatables to send home by one of the men. During the first week of her marriage, the bride is expected to be up before anyone else to light the fire and prepare coffee for the men before they go into the fields, and to cook the hot meal at noon, or in the evening, to show that she is a good housewife.

If a *contadino* is sent away for theft, or any grave misdemeanour, he can sometimes find another *podere* at a distance, but most commonly sinks in the social scale and becomes a *bracciante*, or day labourer, when his lot is miserable enough. Wages in Tuscany vary from one franc twenty to one franc eighty centimes (11*d.* to 1*s.*7*d.*) per day. The day's work begins at sunrise and lasts till sunset, with half an hour's rest for breakfast at eight in the morning, and one hour for lunch at midday, but in the great heat of summer the midday rest is prolonged; the men come earlier and go away later. When the weather is bad they are for days without employment, and where there are many small children the family is often at starvation point. The women in the lower Val d'Arno are universally occupied in straw plaiting, and if very expert, in exceptional years, can for a short time gain as much as threepence a day. But fashion is always changing and new plaits have to be learned, so that the average gain rarely exceeds fifteen centimes, or 1½*d.*, a day. When the Japanese rush hats came into fashion, the misery was great among the poor plaiters, as Leghorn straw hats were almost unsaleable.

You will seldom find an old peasant who can write and read, though some have learnt to sign their names in a sort of hieroglyph. The rising generation are being instructed in a desultory manner, and are wonderfully quick at learning. Every man in the army is forced to learn under penalty of being kept in the ranks until he can read, write, and cipher a little; so that one may say that the army is one vast school. The conscription is, however, a heavy tax, particularly on the agricultural population, and entails great misery. The loss, for three years, of the son, who in many cases is the chief bread-winner for his younger brothers and sisters or for an invalid father, often reduces the family to beggary. I need not add that the loss to the country is enormous. On the other hand, there is no doubt that the army is the great, and probably the only, method of gradually fusing the different Italian races—I had almost said nationalities. Since the Middle Ages the hatred between, not only the different provinces, but the towns and small villages, has always existed, and is still extremely strong. An Italian seldom, in Italy at least, speaks of himself as an Italian, but as a Neapolitan, a Tuscan, a Piedmontese, a Roman, or a Lombard; and he believes his own province has the monopoly of honesty, truth, and exemption from crime. All this will, no doubt, pass when education has had time to influence the lower classes, when the quaint customs of the *contadini* will disappear, as their costume has already done.

It ought to be mentioned that every large estate has *patti colonici*, or bye-laws, of its own. I know of one where the *patti* instituted in 1608 are still followed, and the original document, beautifully written on vellum, hangs in the *fattoria*, or factor's apartments. One peasant of each *podere* is hereby bound to work gratis ten days in the year for the *padrone*, and to do a certain amount of haulage; two women of each family of peasants are to come to the *fattoria* to wash linen one day every three months; at Christmas and at Easter every *podere* must give a pair of capons, and four dozen of eggs during the year as compensation for the damage done by the poultry to the crops, otherwise the *contadino* may only keep three hens; 150 yards of trenching is to be done by the peasant every year for planting vines and olives. By many these *patti* have been condemned as a remnant of feudalism, but, in fact, they are a kind of compensation for what the peasant takes from the land in addition to his lawful half share—vegetables, fruit, milk for the children, etc., which cannot, of course, be divided and are never taken into account.

Though *mezzeria* is undoubtedly a bar to agricultural progress, it establishes a community of interest and kindly relations between proprietor and peasant. Socialism has no followers among the *contadini;* by old-established custom they are helped over a bad year by their *padrone,* who gives them what wheat they need, to be repaid in wine or oil. Like all human institutions, it has two sides, and may be lauded as beneficial and wholesome, or condemned as retrograde. Lately, it has been introduced into some parts of Sicily, where it seems to work well. John Stuart Mill, after weighing the evidence on both sides, remarks in his *Principles of Political Economy,* "The fixity of tenure which the *metayer,* so long as he fulfils his own obligations, possesses by usage, though not by law, gives him the local attachments, and almost the strong sense of personal interest, characteristic of a proprietor."

THE JUBILEE OF A CRUCIFIX

THE month of April will long be remembered by the good people of Signa, for fifty years have passed since the *festa* of the miraculous "Crucifix of Providence" was celebrated at the church of Le Selve.

Standing high above the valley of the Arno, amid elms and cypresses, it adjoins an old monastery of Carmelite friars, suppressed, like so many others, in the time of Napoleon I. Peasant children now play in the picturesque two-storied cloisters; and the monks' garden, with its fine old well, has been turned into a nursery for young olive trees. The refectory is a granary, and the abbot's apartment is inhabited by the little village priest, who ekes out his scanty stipend by embroidering altar cloths and making fireworks for village *fêtes*.

The church, said to have been restored by Buontalenti, has a nave of considerable height and purity of design, terminating in an apse. There are no side chapels, but over one of the altars is a Madonna and Child, of painted *papier-mâché*, which must assuredly have been fashioned by a master hand, for the Virgin is a type of perfect beauty and graciousness. Under the high altar is a small crypt where S. Andrea Corsini celebrated his first mass, and was accepted by Our Lady as her servant. Great preparations had been made in Florence by the great Corsini family for this event, but the young priest fled secretly from the city the preceding day, and took refuge with the friars at Le Selve. He passed the night at prayer in the crypt, and when at daybreak, trembling with religious fervour, he raised the chalice to his lips, Our Lady appeared to him, and smiling, said: *Tu es servus meus.*

The crowd in the church was great, particularly near the high altar, entirely covered with flowers, and resplendent with lights; and on the organ was being played one of Verdi's operas.

As I complimented the plain little curate upon the success of his *festa*, a man pushed in between us, and the priest instantly apostrophised him in one of those old proverbs which all Tuscans have on the tips of their tongues—

"He who has no shame thinks the world is his." Upon which the tall, handsome mason, the Don Juan of the village, looked down upon the shrivelled little man, and replied by another: "Three things are beautiful on this earth—a robed priest, an armed knight, and a bejewelled woman. But," added he, impertinently, "especially the first." Fortunately the little curate was called away to receive the bishop, or the war of words might have ended in broken heads.

VILLA DELLE SELVE

Face page 224

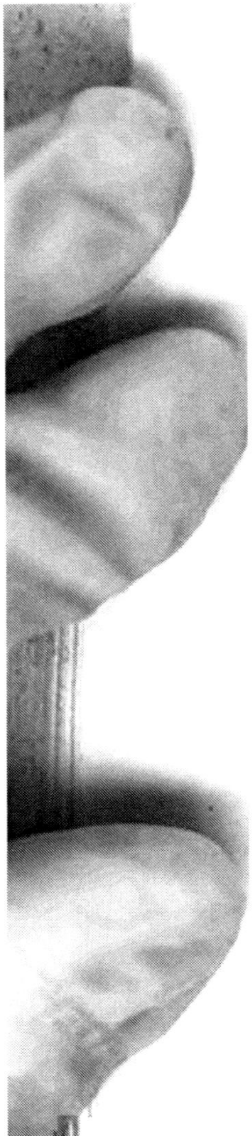

The stately villa of Le Selve, which stands near by the convent, belonged in olden days to the powerful family of the Acciajuoli; but the present building was planned by that great architect, Buontalenti, for the Strozzi, whose arms are to be seen on several tombs in the church. It was purchased afterwards by the Salviati; and one of them, Pilippo, lent it to his "most dear friend" Galileo Galilei, who lived there for six years, and whose discoveries of the revolution of the sun upon its axis, of the sun-spots, of the rings of Saturn, and of the phases of Venus and of Mars, and their rotation round the sun, were made from the upper terrace. A winding staircase led down to his study, where now is the office of the factor, and I congratulated him on inhabiting a room once occupied by so great a man. But he, being an ally of the little priest, disdainfully said: "I think the old proverb is true; from the roof upwards no man knows the distance, or what there is." Galileo's only recreation was working in the garden, and he used to boast of his skill in pruning vines and fruit trees. A wall, with a peculiar curve behind the villa, is said to have been built by him; the faintest whisper is heard distinctly from one end to the other.

From the broad terrace the view is of great extent and of wonderful beauty. "One can see half the world," remarked a peasant beside us. Below us flowed the glinting river, fringed with tall, tendergreen poplars, and opposite the hill of Artimino rose precipitously the golden patches of broom glowing amongst the rocks. It is crowned by the great Medicean villa, Ferdinanda, built for the Grand Duke Ferdinando I. by Buontalenti. Further off to the right, down in the plain, Poggio a Cajano, another Medicean villa, rises like a giant, the tall trees near it look like small shrubs. Giuliano da San Gallo planned it for Lorenzo the Magnificent, and the little stream, Ambra, "loveliest of Cajano's nymphs," as Poliziano calls it, flows through the grounds. Its name is known to all students of Italian literature by the charming poem written by Lorenzo himself. One of the many tragedies of the Medici family took place at Poggio a Cajano, when Francesco de' Medici and his second wife, Bianca Cappello, "the abominable Bianca," as her husband's brother and successor, the Cardinal, called her, died within a few hours of one another. Some say the Cardinal poisoned them; others, that she had prepared a tart for him, of which the Grand Duke ate by mistake, when she, in despair, took the rest; others, again, say they died of tertian fever.

Down, and more to the right again, lies the picturesque old bridge over the river and the grey machicolated walls and towers of Lastra a Signa, built in 1377 by the English *condottiere*, Sir John Hawkwood, as a defence against the Pisans, when he was in the service of the Florentine Republic. On the opposite side of the river is Beata Signa, which takes its name of "blessed" from the humble shepherd-maid, La Beata Giovanna. Many were the miracles she worked in olden days, and now her mummified body lies under the high altar of the old church, and on Easter Monday the "Festa degli Angeli" is held every year in her honour.

This "Festival of the Angels" is one of the prettiest of old-world celebrations, and the confraternities of the country round vie with each other to make a gallant show, as they bring their yearly offering of oil to the shrine of the humble shepherdess. The little processions wind down the lanes with banners flying, and, when they can afford it, a band. A gaily caparisoned donkey carries the oil in two small barrels, slung like panniers, one on either side, and on a platform above them stands the prettiest little girl of the parish, supported by an iron upright with a hoop. Sometimes a pair of white wings are fastened to the child's shoulders; she is crowned with roses and many pearl *vezzi*, or necklaces, and she holds an olive branch in her tiny hands. One after another the processions file into the old church, waving their banners while the band plays its loudest, and at the tomb the little girl is lifted off the donkey and presents the oil to the Beata Giovanni. Occasionally an ill-behaved donkey brays aloud in the church, to the confusion of his owner and the great amusement of the crowd.

But we must return to Le Selve, where preparations were being made for the long-expected procession of the Crucifix of Providence, whose Christ is fashioned in *papier-mâché*, like the lovely Madonna in the church. Slowly the long line of chanting priests, small acolytes in snow-white robes, and stalwart men bearing the great crucifix, banners, and canopies, came out of the church and wended their way down the steep road, strewn with rose leaves, irises, and sweet herbs, to Ponte a Signa.

In the soft opalescent light of an Italian spring evening it returned, winding slowly with flaring torches, like a huge fiery serpent beneath the olives and the cypresses. As the stars appeared the peasants lit up their houses, and the stately old villa became a blaze of light.

We walked home with some peasant friends, and startled the nightingales and the little assiola owls by singing *stornelli*—

"Flower of the night
When you pass, the grass springs 'neath your treading so light,
And the May month blooms forth to gladden our sight.

"Flower of the sward
In my heart I have locked up full many a word;
I am sure you will shed tears when they are all heard.

"Flower of the wold
Love's prisoner am I when your face I behold;
Your beauty and grace by no tongue can be told.

THE JUBILEE OF A CRUCIFIX

"Flower of the cane
Your sweet pretty face is a picture I swear:
You're made all of manna and sugarcane rare.

"Flower of the spring
Of all the fair flow'rets that flower in May,
The flower of my love shall be the most gay.

"Flower of the rose
A nosegay rare I bind, and to the market take,
I feign to hate thee, darling, while love mine heart doth break."

PLYMOUTH
WILLIAM BRENDON AND SON
PRINTERS

13

LaVergne, TN USA
02 February 2011
214989LV00004B/24/P

9 781141 151882